Whirlpool
Home Appliances

Micro Menus
Cookbook®

BETTER HOMES AND GARDENS
TEST KITCHEN™

This seal assures you that every recipe in Micro Menus Cookbook has been tested in the Better Homes and Gardens® Test Kitchen. This means that each recipe is practical and reliable, and meets our high standards of taste appeal.

Pictured on the cover: Salisbury Steak (See recipe, page 44.)

The trademarks WHIRLPOOL, Whirlpool and Whirlpool® are property of Whirlpool Corporation, Benton Harbor, Michigan 49022.

Part No. 4B73533A/4158272 Rev. A

NOTE: Be sure you carefully read and understand the Use and Care booklet that came with your microwave oven before starting to use the oven. It contains operating instructions, safety recommendations, and other important information about the proper use of your microwave oven.

PRECAUTIONS TO AVOID POSSIBLE EXPOSURE TO EXCESSIVE MICROWAVE ENERGY

- Do not attempt to operate this oven with the door open since open-door operation can result in harmful exposure to microwave energy. It is important not to defeat or tamper with the safety interlocks.
- Do not place any object between the oven front face and the door or allow soil or cleaner residue to accumulate on sealing surfaces.
- Do not operate the oven if it is damaged. It is particularly important that the oven door close properly and that there is no damage to the: (1) door (bent), (2) hinges and latches (broken or loosened), (3) door seals and sealing surfaces.
- The oven should not be adjusted or repaired by anyone except properly qualified service personnel.
- The oven should be checked for microwave leakage by qualified service personnel after a repair is made.
- Do not operate the oven if the door glass is broken.
- Do not operate the microwave oven with the outer cabinet removed.

IF YOU NEED SERVICE OR ASSISTANCE, WE SUGGEST YOU FOLLOW THESE 4 STEPS.

1. Before calling for assistance*...

Check the things you can do yourself. Refer to the literature furnished with your appliance to ensure it is correctly installed and you are familiar with its normal operation.

2. If you need assistance*...

Call Whirlpool Consumer Assistance Center telephone number. Dial free from anywhere in the U.S.:

1-800-253-1301

and talk with one of our trained consultants. The consultant can instruct you in how to obtain satisfactory operation from your appliance or, if service is necessary, recommend a qualified service company in your area.

If you prefer, write to:
Mr. Donald Skinner
Director of Consumer Relations
Whirlpool Corporation
2000 M-63
Benton Harbor, MI 49022

Please include a daytime phone number in your correspondence.

3. If you need service*...

Whirlpool has a nationwide network of authorized Whirlpool^{SM} service companies. Whirlpool service technicians are trained to fulfill the product warranty and provide after-warranty service, anywhere in the Unitied States. To locate the authorized Whirlpool service company in your area, call our Consumer Assistance Center telephone number (see Step 2) or look in your telephone directory Yellow Pages under:

APPLIANCES–HOUSEHOLD–
MAJOR–SERVICE & REPAIR

ELECTRICAL APPLIANCES–
MAJOR–REPAIRING & PARTS

OR

WASHING MACHINES, DRYERS
& IRONERS–SERVICING
WHIRLPOOL APPLIANCES
AUTHORIZED WHIRLPOOL SERVICE

SERVICE COMPANIES
XYZ SERVICE CO.
123 MAPLE 999-9999

4. If you are not satisfied with how the problem was solved*...

- Contact the Major Appliance Consumer Action Panel (MACAP). MACAP is a group of independent consumer experts that voices consumer views at the highest levels of the major appliance industry.
- Contact MACAP only when the dealer, authorized servicer or Whirlpool have failed to resolve your problem.

  Major Appliance Consumer Action Panel
  20 North Wacker Drive
  Chicago, IL 60606

- MACAP will in turn inform us of your action.

* When requesting assistance, please provide: model number, serial number, date of purchase, and a complete description of the problem. This information is needed in order to better respond to your request.

TABLE OF CONTENTS

Welcome to Microwave Cooking

It's exciting to cook delicious meals with ease and speed in a Whirlpool microwave oven! Your Whirlpool Micro Menus Cookbook was written especially with you in mind. It features dozens of great-tasting recipes and more than 130 colorful how-to photographs guaranteed to make microwave cooking a breeze. For newcomers to microwave cooking, or for a simple refresher course for the experienced microwave cook, the ABC's chapter will start you off on a rewarding partnership with your microwave oven. And, there's lots more! You'll find recipes for sure-to-please family favorites and company's-coming specialties. There are handy kitchen tips galore and easy-to-read charts for defrosting foods, roasting meats, cooking vegetables, and cooking packaged convenience foods. Plus, guidelines for bi-level cooking and lessons on converting conventional recipes to timesaving microwave recipes will allow you to prepare your favorites in minutes. So turn the page and discover for yourself the speed and convenience of microwave cooking.

The ABC's of Microwave Cooking

The fascinating world of microwave cooking is at your fingertips. And we've made it easy for you to learn the hows and whys of microwaving with color photographs and clearly written information. Once you've mastered the basics, enjoy preparing the many delicious recipes developed especially with you in mind!

The ABC's of Microwave Cooking

Meet the microwave

"Micro" means tiny, very small, short. In the case of microwaves, we're talking about short energy waves. Microwaves are non-ionizing electromagnetic waves. You're more familiar with energy waves than you may think. A bass drum produces relatively long energy waves. Waves become progressively shorter as we go from the drum to the piccolo to radio waves to visible light waves.

Waves of different lengths have different characteristics. Holding up your hand won't stop sound waves, but it can stop light waves. You use different kinds of energy waves every day. But, right now let's think only about microwaves.

Cooking power of microwaves

Microwaves have three important characteristics:

1. Microwaves are reflected off metals.
2. Microwaves pass through most glass, paper, and plastic objects.
3. Microwaves are absorbed by food.

When microwaves are absorbed by food, what happens? The molecules in the food begin to vibrate. The vibrating molecules bump into each other causing friction. This friction produces heat instantly within the food. You can get an idea of heat produced by friction by rubbing your hands together quickly.

How does microwave cooking differ from conventional cooking? With conventional range cooking, you heat the air in the oven. The hot air heats the surface of the food. From here, the heat is conducted slowly to the inside of the food.

Microwaves also cook food from the outside in. The greatest amount of microwave energy is absorbed near the surface of the food. Where this absorption occurs, cooking begins immediately. The waves lose power as they go deeper into the food. That's why more cooking takes place at a depth of 1 to 2 inches.

Thin foods cook fairly rapidly and evenly throughout, but thicker foods, such as roasts, cook faster in areas nearest the surface where microwaves are absorbed. The center of the roast cooks by conduction of heat, which is much slower. Remember, heat is produced only in the food, not in the cavity of the microwave oven.

Microwave cooking can burn

Be careful when you're removing dishes and other food containers from the microwave oven. They may get hot enough that you will need to use hot pads.

Use caution when removing a cover. Steam builds up in the container and can burn you.

Cook foods according to the times and quantities given in the cookbook. And do not overcook foods or they may burn. Shorten the cooking time for smaller quantities. As in conventional cooking, overcooking will burn food and food may flame. A microwave oven is different from a conventional oven. For best results, use the cookbook directions.

Think "time"

Time is the main consideration, when cooking in a microwave oven, rather than both time and temperature as in conventional cooking. These five factors affect your cooking time.

1. Starting temperature.

It's reassuring to know that even with the speed of microwaves, warm water still comes to a boil faster than cold water. Likewise, refrigerated foods take longer to heat than the same foods starting at room temperature. These considerations become more important due to the speed with which food cooks in the microwave oven.

Feel free to substitute a canned product for a frozen one, but remember to reduce the cooking time when you do.

2. Quantity of food.

When the *amount* of food varies, the *cooking time* varies also. For example, 1 potato may take 4 minutes to bake while 2 potatoes take 7 minutes. Likewise, 1 cup of cool tap water boils in about 2 minutes 30 seconds but 2 cups take approximately 4 minutes 30 seconds. (Note that cooking time does not exactly double as food mass doubles.)

Here are some rules of thumb to follow when you adjust a recipe. Remember when cooking smaller amounts of food that *half* the quantity doesn't necessarily cook in *half* the time. Instead, we suggest that you reduce the time by slightly less than half. Then check for doneness, and add a little more cooking time if nec-

essary. To double a recipe add a little more than half the original cooking time. Check for doneness, and then add more time in small portions if necessary.

3. Shape of the food.

Thinner foods cook faster in the microwave oven than thicker foods. Why? Remember microwaves penetrate to a depth of 3/4 to 2 inches (depending on the food) and lose power as they penetrate more deeply. Therefore, thinner foods and outside layers of thicker foods are cooked by microwaves while the center of thicker foods is cooked by slower conduction of heat.

4. Composition of the food.

Some foods cook faster than others because of ingredients they contain. For example, a food containing large amounts of sugar or fat will heat faster than a food with little sugar or fat.

5. Density of the food.

Two foods of the same weight will take different heating and cooking times because there may be more air between the molecules of one. So, a roast will take longer to cook than the same weight of rolls.

Microwave-safe labels

Look for labels on cooking utensils that indicate they are safe to use in the microwave oven. Terms like "microwave oven safe" or "recommended for microwave ovens" may appear on the label or sticker, or be printed on the dish itself.

Do NOT home can

All potentially harmful micro-organisms must be killed when canning foods. Microwave cooking does not reach the high temperatures needed. When home canning, you will destroy harmful bacteria by cooking foods at temperatures well above boiling (212°F) in a pressure cooker.

Foods high in acid, while acceptable for water bath canning at boiling temperatures, must still be held at boiling temperatures for specified lengths of time. For these foods a conventional water bath canner is best because it allows jars of food to be submerged in boiling water to assure constant heat to each jar during canning.

Cook power control

The control on your microwave oven is easy to use. Its operation is similar to the control knob on surface units of your range. For example, a **Low** setting means low power and slow cooking.

For the quick heating of convenience foods, beverages, vegetables, fruits, burgers, cupcakes, and sauces, use **High Power.** Choose **Medium High or Cook Power 7 (70%)** for cooking tender meats, poultry, meat loaves, and casseroles that require quick cooking to retain moisture and tenderness. Use **Medium or Cook Power 5 (50%)** for less-tender meats that need to simmer, such as pot roast and stew, or for even cooking of baked goods such as cakes. **Low or Cook Power 2 (20%)** is best for softening butter, raising yeast breads, and holding foods at serving temperature.

Some foods can be cooked at more than one power setting. Foods can be thawed quickly at **High Power** or **Medium High or Cook Power 7 (70%)**, but need more watching and care than the same item done at **Low or Cook Power 2 (20%)**, or **Medium Low or Cook Power 3 (30%)**.

Reheating foods can also be done at a wide range of settings. You can reheat quickly at **High Power** but open the door and stir, turn, or rotate the food a few times while it's heating.

On the other hand, you can reheat items more evenly at a lower setting--without as much stirring--but it will take a slightly longer heating time.

You can roast at **High Power** but you will need to check and reposition the food periodically to ensure even cooking. A lower setting for roasting requires less watching, but it will take a longer time to cook. Use the setting and method that fits best into your schedule.

The wide variety of Cook Power control settings allows for cooking versatility. Use good cooking sense. Turn the power down if food is cooking too quickly. Use a higher setting and stir a few times if you want a casserole to heat more quickly. If you consistently need to cook foods longer than the recipe states, your voltage may be low--try cooking at the next highest power level. The recipes are a guideline. You'll find specific settings mentioned in each recipe. We found these settings gave the best results when we prepared the recipes in the *Better Homes and Gardens® Test Kitchens.*

COOK POWER	LEVELS
High Power =	100% of Full Power
9 =	90% of Full Power
8 =	80% of Full Power
(Med. High) 7 =	70% of Full Power
6 =	60% of Full Power
(Medium) 5 =	50% of Full Power
4 =	40% of Full Power
(Med. Low) 3 =	30% of Full Power
2 =	20% of Full Power
(Low) 1 =	10% of Full Power
0 =	0% of Full Power

Cook with confidence

Every recipe begins with total cooking time. Variable cook power levels are shown in bold type so they are easy to read. You'll also find directions for selecting proper utensils, covering, and stirring to ensure a delicious recipe every time you cook.

Recipes have been tested for consistent results and quality. However, it's a good idea to visually check for doneness shortly before the recommended cooking time is up to avoid overcooking. Remember, a few minutes in the microwave oven at High Power is equal to about four times the conventional cooking time. Therefore, overcooking can happen quickly. Remember to add more cooking time in small amounts (1 minute or less) and check for doneness.

Glossary of microwave terms

Absorption--One of the basic characteristics of microwaves referred to in microwave cooking. Microwaves are absorbed by foods and they cause certain molecules in the food to vibrate very rapidly. As the molecules vibrate, they bump into each other. Friction results from this vibration and heat is produced.

Adapting Conventional Recipes-Most recipes can be adapted with some alterations. Microwaves cook food 3 to 4 times faster; follow directions for a similar microwave recipe for best results. (See the chapter on Converting Recipes.)

Arcing--A sparking or lightning-like effect that can be seen and heard when metal is improperly used in the microwave oven.

Arranging--The placement of the food in the cooking utensil or microwave oven to give best cooking results for that food. For example, arrange custard cups in a circle instead of in rows.

Bi-Level Cooking--Is the cooking process done on a second level by placing food on a removable rack. Allows cooking of more than one food item at one time, with dishes placed both on the rack and the bottom oven shelf.

Cook Power Levels--Are used to adjust the speed which foods cook. A similar principle is heat on a conventional range. Foods such as cakes and slow cooking meats can be started on Low or High and changed partway through cooking.

Covering--A technique used to prevent spattering and retain moisture and heat to ensure even cooking.

Defrosting--Using microwave energy to quickly break down ice crystals in a frozen food. Some foods defrost quickly and evenly, while others require turning so outer edges do not begin to cook before the center is thawed. (See specific chapters for more detailed defrosting directions.)

Density--Foods have different densities and absorb microwaves at different rates. Porous foods, such as breads, absorb microwaves easily, but dense, compact foods, such as meats, absorb microwaves on the exterior and heat is transferred to the center by conduction.

Effective Wattage--A measure of microwave oven power output at other than a High setting. It's the result achieved by cycling the magnetron tube on and off. The amount of time the tube is on determines "effective wattage" available for cooking at a particular variable cook power setting. For example, in a 650 watt oven at a Cook Power of Medium (50%), the power is on $\frac{1}{2}$ of the time. The result would be an "effective wattage" of 325 watts.

Holding Time--Refer to Standing Time.

Magnetron Tube--The "heart" of the microwave oven. It is a vacuum tube that produces microwave energy.

Meal Sensor Temperature Probe--See Temperature Probe.

Microwave--Term meaning high-frequency wave of energy.

Overcooking--Not always visible, but can cause drying, hard spots, toughening, and the separation of sauces. It occurs when food cooks too long. Remember, foods continue to cook after removal from oven, so allow for standing time.

Piercing--To break food membrane or slit plastic covering to allow steam to escape.

Rearranging--To reposition. This technique is used for foods that can't be stirred and helps distribute heat. Same principle as stirring, turning food, and turning dish.

Rotating--A quarter- or half-turn of the dish. Technique used for foods that can't be stirred, turned over, or rearranged.

Shielding--Using small pieces of foil to cover small areas of a large or uneven food to prevent it from overcooking.

Standing Time--Step used in both defrosting food and cooking food. It is the time necessary to equalize temperature in food *after* defrosting and *before* cooking (holding time). Term also refers to the time after a food has cooked that allows for equalization of heat and cooking doneness throughout the food. Most recipes that suggest a "standing time" are those for dense foods or larger amounts of food. The process requires removing the food from the oven and covering it with aluminum foil to help retain the heat. The food is allowed to rest for 5 to 15 minutes, depending on the type and quantity of food cooked. This standing time permits the heat created on the outer layers to be conducted toward the center, for more even cooking inside.

Stirring--The redistributing of the food in a cooking utensil by moving hot food from the outer edge to the center.

Temperature Probe--The device used to cook food to a pre-set internal temperature rather than cooking for a set time. One end of the probe plugs in the side wall of oven cavity. The temperature sensing end is put into the food being cooked. When the probe senses the set temperature, the oven shuts off automatically and an end-of-cycle signal sounds.

Turning--Inverting food during cooking, such as a roast, or rotating a dish for foods that cannot be stirred, such as cake.

Undercooking--Step used when cooking food to an almost-done state, and then allowing for the standing time to complete the cooking.

Volume--The amount of food that will affect the length of cooking time. Certain types of foods need extra space to expand during cooking. For example, cakes rise higher than those that are conventionally-baked, and milk-based foods and candies will rise and possibly boil over if not placed in a container that is 3 to 4 times larger than the amount of food. The concentration of the microwaves decreases as the volume of the food increases, therefore the cooking time increases.

Utensils

More and more households are cooking with microwave ovens, and the microwave utensil industry is growing to accommodate the consumer. In addition to items designed for microwave cooking, many familiar conventional utensils are equally suitable for microwave cooking. Select the right cooking utensil for each job.

Shape

Select round-shaped dishes to ensure the even cooking of food. Because microwaves penetrate foods to about 1 inch from top, bottom, and sides, losing power the deeper they go, round-shaped dishes allow areas of the food to cook evenly.

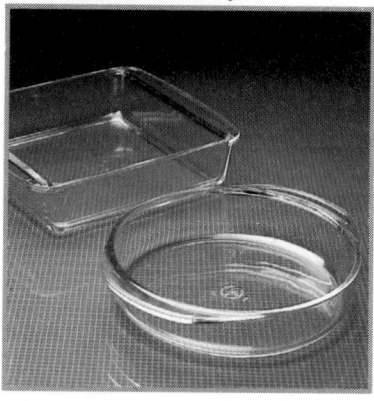

Shape

Make your own ring-shaped dish by placing a custard cup or drinking glass in the center of a round baking dish. Keeping food away from the center of the dish, food will cook more evenly.

Shape

Ring molds and fluted ring baking dishes enable the microwaves to penetrate food equally from all directions.

Shape

Choose dishes with straight sides to help keep the food more evenly distributed. If a dish has shallow areas the food will be less concentrated and will have a tendency to overcook.

11

Depth

The depth of the dish is as important as its capacity in assuring even cooking. The food cooked in a shallow 2-quart dish compared with food cooked in a deep 2-quart dish will cook at different rates depending upon the density of the food. Follow the directions in the recipe for suggested cooking dishes.

Dish test

If you are not certain that a glass, pottery, or china dish is microwave-safe, use this simple test. Pour some cold water into a glass measure. Set it inside or beside the dish you wish to test. Cook in the microwave oven for 1 minute at High Power. If the water is warm but the dish remains cool, the dish can be used for microwave cooking. If the water is warm and the dish feels lukewarm, the dish is suitable only for heating or reheating food. However, if the water stays cool while the dish becomes hot, don't use the dish in your microwave for any purpose.

This test is not satisfactory for plastic containers, since most plastics are transparent to microwaves. Distortion of some plastics is due to contact with hot food, not microwave energy.

Size

Dish size affects the way food cooks, the cooking time, and frequency of cooking attention needed. As shown here, cooking a small amount of food closely contained in a custard cup makes more efficient use of microwaves and will cook the food faster because it is more closely contained than if it was spread out in a large baking dish.

Covers

Covers are used in the microwave oven either to absorb moisture or grease or to keep moisture and heat near the food. If your casserole dish has a glass or pottery lid, you can use it in the microwave. If your dish has no cover, glass plates and saucers, plastic wrap, waxed paper, and even paper toweling can serve as a cover or partial cover, depending on the food and length of time you're cooking.

Household paper products

Microwaves will pass through most paper containers. Some of the typical paper products to use include paper plates, napkins, cups, and toweling; freezer paper; baking parchment; waxed paper; and paper from frozen food packages.

Paper towels (white and unpatterned) help absorb grease or moisture and help to prevent spattering. Remember, use of paper should be limited to cooking times up to 4 minutes (except when cooking up to 8 slices of bacon) or frozen food cooking times up to 10 minutes.

Glass and ceramics

These are among the most useful of microwave utensils. You'll notice that you already have many of them for use in conventional cooking. With a microwave oven, you can measure, mix, and cook in only one glass measuring cup. Clear glass baking dishes allow you to check for doneness on the bottom of cakes, pies, and breads. Look for labels on the utensils that indicate they are recommended for microwave oven use. Also, avoid using chipped or cracked utensils in the microwave oven.

Special paper products

These are some examples of paper products especially designed for use in the microwave oven. Plastic-coated divided trays and different sizes of storage containers are handy for heating and serving most foods. The disposable roasting rack makes cleanup a snap.

Glass and china to avoid

Do not use glass or ceramic dishes with metallic trim or metal bands. The metal may arc, blacken, or overheat the area next to it and crack the dish. And don't use utensils with metal handles, screws, or other metal parts that cannot be removed.

Pottery

Many plates and serving dishes make good microwave utensils. But be sure the dish can withstand high temperatures. Porcelain and stoneware are good choices because they're usually conventional ovenproof, too.

Special plastic products

There are many specially designed plastic cooking dishes and utensils for the microwave oven. These attractive accessories include stirring utensils, roasting racks, cupcake holders, cake dishes, and fluted tube cake pans.

Household plastic products

Some plastics are transparent to microwaves, but vary in temperatures they can withstand. Some are suitable for heating but will melt or distort during cooking. Read the manufacturer's directions carefully and use the product only for foods recommended. Common plastics include boil-in-the-bag pouches, oven-cooking bags, and microwave-safe plastic wrap. Styrofoam™ utensils are suitable for heating foods to serving temperature, but distort at 170°F. Most tableware plastics can be used for heating foods to a serving temperature of 140°F.

Plastic products to avoid

There are many popular and attractive plastic utensils available today, but be cautious as some plastics may melt or soften from the heat of the food. Don't use plastic containers when cooking foods high in fat or sugar, unless recommended by the manufacturer. Lightweight freezer containers may distort because of high food temperatures and should not be used. Do not use melamine utensils and dishes. Also, don't use thin plastic sandwich bags.

Wood and straw

Use wood and straw products for short term heating and cooking. Straw and wood will dry out and may crack from long cooking times or continued use. Remember to select items without metal wires or metallic trim. Typical utensils include wooden skewers and small wooden picks, woven straw baskets, wooden bowls, spoons, and platters.

Metal products to avoid

Metal can cause arcing--a sparking, lightninglike effect. This can pit oven walls or cause fire within the utensil or the food. Do not use metal or part-metal pans; standard meat or candy thermometers; frozen dinner trays with sides over ¾ inch high; or glass, paper, or ceramic containers with metallic trim or metal bands. Remove all twist ties, too.

Metals

Metal reflects microwave energy so it can't penetrate the food. The reflective properties of a metal can sometimes be used to an advantage. Strips of foil will act as a "shield" during defrosting and cooking, so one area of the food won't overcook.

Frozen entrées in shallow foil pans will heat evenly from the top only, without overcooking the corners and sides.

Use only thermometers that have been specially designed for use in the microwave oven.

Accurate temperature reading

Specially designed microwave meat and candy thermometers are available for use in microwave oven cooking. However, conventional thermometers cannot be used in microwave ovens because the mercury reflects the microwaves resulting in inaccurate readings.

Temperature probes are standard cooking equipment with many microwave ovens. When the food reaches a preset internal temperature, the probe turns the oven off.

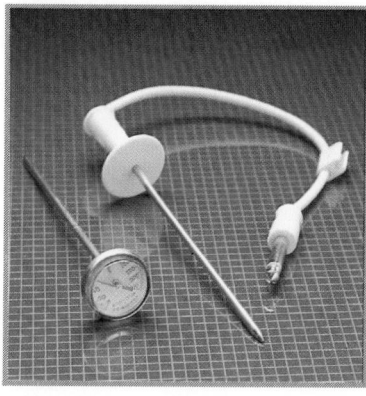

Temperature probe

The microwave temperature probe is designed to automatically turn the microwave oven off when the food has reached the right temperature. So instead of cooking by time, you can now cook by temperature. This helps prevent overcooking and helps eliminate the guesswork of cooking times. To coordinate the cooking times for meals, recipes in this book give both temperature and timings. If your oven comes with a temperature probe, follow these instructions:

First, insert the probe into the center of the food. Then plug the probe's other end into the receptacle on the inside of the oven. Remember, the first third of the probe must be stuck into the food to ensure an accurate temperature reading. If the microwave oven turns off unusually early, it may mean the probe has slipped out of place or needs to be more accurately positioned. Simply relocate the probe and continue cooking. Do not use the probe in pork or poultry recipes.

Beef roasts

For beef roasts, completely defrost before roasting. The probe must be positioned in the center of the largest muscle, not touching fat or bone. Cook to 130° to 145°F at Cook Power 7 (70%).

Cover roast with foil after removing from the microwave oven for 10 minutes to ensure more even final cooking.

Meat loaf

Cook your family's favorite meat loaf to an internal temperature of 170°F at Cook Power 7 (70%). Position the probe in the center of the meat loaf. Let stand 5 minutes before serving.

If the recipe contains pork, do not use the temperature probe.

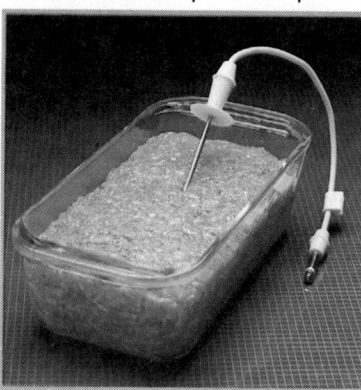

Casseroles

Place the probe into the center of the casserole. Cook the mixture to about 165°F at Cook Power 7 (70%). Stir once or twice for more even cooking.

Liquids

For liquids such as syrup and soup, cook to about 165°F at High Power.

Browning dish

Ceramic browning utensils are available in several sizes and styles. A special coating of tin oxide on the bottom absorbs microwave energy. After it is pre-heated, the dish will sear, brown, stir-fry, or grill food.

Follow these tips for using the microwave browning dish:

1. Do not preheat the dish for more than 8 minutes.

2. Use hot pads when handling the browning dish.

3. Preheat the browning dish empty and uncovered.

4. Do not use non-stick vegetable coatings with the dish.

5. Cover the dish with the glass lid to prevent excessive spattering and to help foods cook more quickly and evenly.

6. If you remove the preheated dish from the oven, set it on a heat-resistant surface to avoid any damage to your countertop.

Wash your browning dish in the dishwasher or by hand in hot sudsy water. Do not use harsh cleaning pads such as steel wool--you may scratch the dish.

Frying

Fry desired number of chicken pieces quickly and easily in the browning dish. With the browning dish you only use a tablespoon of cooking oil and the natural chicken juices are sealed in because it browns so quickly.

Stir-frying

Stir-fried vegetables are a snap in the browning dish. Cooked to the crisp-tender stage, you only have to stir once or twice; and they retain their bright fresh color, too!

Grilling

French toast grills to a crisp golden brown in about 1 minute. And you can grill your favorite sandwich in a matter of seconds, too. Other breakfast and brunch foods that you would serve browned include hearty omelets and hash.

Preheat it first!

Preheat your browning dish at High Power without the lid for the time specified. Then add oil, if directed. Add food and cook as directed. To cook more than one batch, preheat the browning dish between each batch for about half the original preheating time specified.

Food Characteristics

Food size, shape, temperature, quantity, and composition all affect the cooking time. Let's take a closer look; knowing what factors affect speed and cooking evenness will let you enjoy all the advantages of microwave cooking.

Size and shape

Notice the variety of food sizes and shapes. Food size, shape, and composition can make important differences in cooking time and cooking evenness of the food.

Shape

Foods that are shaped in ring molds or other round shapes (such as ground meat patties) will cook more evenly than square, oblong, or irregular-shaped foods since microwaves penetrate equally from all sides.

Shape

Here is a common example of a piece of meat that has varying thicknesses and jagged, uneven corners. Try to choose a pot roast that has the same thickness throughout. Similar to conventional cooking, a roast which is thinner at one end will be done first in that area. Cooking times are affected by the evenness of the cut and you run the risk of overcooking the food when there are any uneven, unprotected areas. Shield any area that is cooking faster than other areas.

Starting temperature

The starting temperature of most foods affects the total recipe cooking time. Remember, refrigerated foods take longer to heat than the same foods starting at room temperature. We have tested our recipes with ingredients taken directly from their proper storage. So if you substitute a frozen product for a canned product, you will need to increase the cooking time.

Density

These two foods may weigh the same, but more dense foods (like a ham slice) will take longer to cook or heat than more porous foods like bread, cake, or rolls.

Fat content

Trim and discard excess fat. The amount and distribution of fat affects the way meat cooks. The more evenly distributed, the more evenly it will cook. Fat helps tenderize meat, too.

Quantity

When the amount of food varies, the cooking time varies also. For example, 1 cupcake may take 30 to 35 seconds to bake, while 6 cupcakes take about 2 minutes 30 seconds. Likewise, 1 cup of cool tap water boils in about 2 minutes 30 seconds—but 2 cups take approximately 4 minutes 30 seconds.

Bone content

Boneless cuts of meat cook more slowly but more evenly than meats containing bones. Similar to conventional cooking, the meat next to the bone in dense foods will take longer to cook. It's especially important in pork chops and ribs to check these areas for thorough doneness; add more cooking time, if necessary. In less dense, bony foods such as chicken legs, the bony areas will cook faster than more dense areas. Shield bony areas to prevent overcooking.

Sugar content

You'll find some foods cook faster than others because of the ingredients they contain. Take a jelly-filled sweet roll or doughnut, for example. After heating, the doughnut may feel cool to the touch while the sugary jelly inside the doughnut may be very hot. Foods high in sugar or fat content heat faster than other foods.

Prick to release pressure

Potatoes, chicken livers, and eggs are examples of foods that are tightly covered by a natural skin or membrane. Steam builds up pressure in these foods and therefore they must be pricked before cooking in the microwave oven to prevent bursting.

Moisture content

Moisture content of foods affects cooking results too. Because foods retain moisture during cooking, little evaporation occurs. In sugary products such as cakes, there is no surrounding heat for the setting of a crust, so it will not brown, but instead, a few moist spots may appear on the surface of the cake. These moist spots will evaporate on standing.

Careful, it may be hot!

Even though microwave cooking is sometimes called "cool cooking," heat conduction from the food may make the container hot enough so that you need to use hot pads.

Be careful when removing a lid or wrapping, no matter what type of utensil you are using. Steam builds up in a container during cooking, so always tilt the lid away from you, poke a hole in a paper or plastic cover, or remove a cover so the steam escapes away from you.

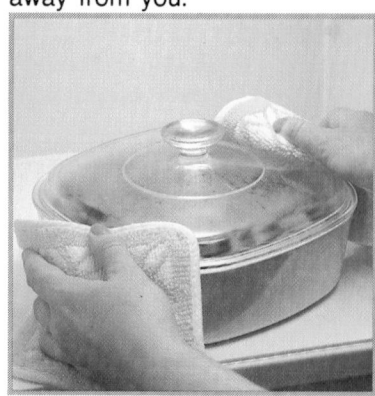

Techniques

Many microwave cooking techniques are familiar to you from conventional cooking. Others are unique to microwaving. All of them speed cooking and equalize heat to help the food cook evenly. Since microwaves penetrate the surfaces of food, the outside areas absorb more energy than the center. By using techniques that equalize heat, you can make sure that all parts of the food are done at the same time.

Covering

Use plastic wrap for a tight covering that will hold in steam and heat. Vent the cover by making a slit in the surface or turn back one edge of the wrap so excess steam will escape and not split the covering.

Covering

The dish you are cooking with may have its own cover. It can be used instead of plastic wrap to trap steam for cooking and keep foods moist.

Covering

A loose cover made with waxed paper will heat foods without steaming. Waxed paper also prevents spattering in the oven.

Covering

Paper toweling or a paper napkin acts as a porous cover to absorb moisture trapped between the food and oven floor. Here, it is used to keep bread surfaces dry.

Covering

An oven cooking bag is used to tenderize and cook meat by holding in the steam. Remember, remove any foil from the bag before using it in the microwave oven. Discard the metal twist tie. Instead, tie loosely with string, leaving a small space for the escape of steam.

Turning/ rotating the dish

Some foods cannot be stirred, rearranged, or turned over. So for foods such as lasagna, meat loaf, and cakes, rotate the baking dish a quarter- or half-turn in the microwave oven after part of the cooking time has elapsed. Follow recipe directions for specific instructions.

Stirring

Stir from the outside in. In conventional cooking, you stir a cheese sauce to keep it from scorching on the bottom of the hot pan. Food in the microwave oven is heated directly by the microwaves, so there's little chance of scorching the bottom. You stir for a different reason. Microwaves cook food from the outside in. Therefore, when you stir you are redistributing the heat—moving the hot outside sauce inward to replace the cooler sauce in the center of the dish.

Stir to distribute heat.

Turning the food

In any microwave oven, there are areas that receive less energy than others. Therefore, turning over or rearranging foods such as roasts and whole vegetables moves them to a new energy pattern and helps all parts cook evenly.

Turn foods that can not be stirred.

Arranging in the oven

It's natural to place a single item in the center of the oven, but when you are cooking several pieces of food, like baking potatoes and cupcakes, arrange them in a ring. Allow space between them, and leave the center open so microwave energy can penetrate from all sides.

Arrange dishes or food in a ring with thin parts to center, or center empty.

Shielding

This technique protects areas that absorb the most energy so the rest of the food can catch up. The most common method is to use strips of foil to shield the top of a large roast, the wing tips of poultry, or the ends of a loaf dish. Another way to shield is to cover meat with a sauce or vegetables.

Shield with pieces of foil to prevent overcooking.

Arranging in the dish

Take advantage of the fact that the center of a dish receives less energy than the outside. And irregularly-shaped foods tend to cook less evenly. So, arrange the food so that bony tips of drumsticks and pork chops, the thin or delicate tails of fish fillets, or the tips of asparagus spears, are in the center, with thick or tough parts near the outside.

Standing time

Standing time, or holding time, is probably the most important of all cooking techniques, but it takes place after microwaving. By allowing foods to stand, you make sure that they are fully cooked but not overcooked.

Large or dense foods, like roasts, need the most standing time. If you microwave a potato until the center is soft, the outside will be mushy. When you're planning a meal, allow enough time for foods that need to stand. Use that time to microwave-cook another food.

Let stand to complete cooking and develop flavor.

Heating

Your microwave oven not only speeds up cooking, but can free you from time-consuming steps in recipe preparation, too. Don't confine your use of this valuable cooking appliance to "microwave recipes"—use it to shortcut cooking methods in all your food preparation.

Softening

To soften ice cream, heat ½ gallon hard-frozen ice cream at Low or Cook Power 2 (20%) for 1 minute 30 seconds to 2 minutes to soften enough to scoop or stir in additional ingredients.

To soften butter or margarine, warm ½ cup (1 stick) unwrapped chilled butter, uncovered, at Low or Cook Power 2 (20%) for 45 to 60 seconds. Warm 1 minute 30 seconds to 2 minutes, if frozen.

Softening

To soften cream cheese, place unwrapped cheese in bowl; heat, uncovered, at Low or Cook Power 2 (20%) for 1 minute for 3-ounce size, 2 minutes 15 seconds for 8-ounce size.

To soften cheese spread, place 8-ounce jar of cheese spread (at room temperature with lid removed) in microwave oven. Heat at Low or Cook Power 2 (20%) for 2 minutes 30 seconds. For a 5-ounce jar, heat uncovered, at Low or Cook Power 2 (20%) for 2 minutes.

Melting

To melt butter or margarine place ½ cup (1 stick) unwrapped chilled butter in bowl. Heat, uncovered, at High for 1 minute 30 seconds. For ¼ cup butter, heat 35 seconds in a custard cup; for 2 tablespoons, heat 30 seconds.

Melting

Unlike melting chocolates conventionally, chocolate melted in the microwave oven will retain its shape until stirred. Follow times given to prevent burning.

To melt semisweet chocolate pieces, place 6 ounces of chocolate pieces in large custard cup. Heat pieces, uncovered, at High for 1 minute 30 seconds. For unsweetened chocolate, place a 1-ounce square of chocolate in a custard cup. Heat, uncovered, at High for 1 minute 15 seconds.

For caramels, place the unwrapped caramels from a 14-ounce package in 1-quart mixing bowl. Warm, uncovered, at High for 2 minutes 15 seconds, stirring often after 1 minute.

Warming baby food

To warm a baby bottle, remove top and nipple; warm an 8-ounce bottle of milk at High for 45 to 60 seconds. Replace top and nipple; shake. Read label directions on jar for heating baby food; stir.

Toasting

To toast 1 cup nuts, spread in pie plate. Cook at High for 5 to 6 minutes till golden, stirring after each minute.

To toast ½ cup coconut, place the coconut in a large custard cup. Cook at High for 2 minutes to 2 minutes 15 seconds till golden, stirring the coconut every 20 seconds.

To toast ¼ cup sesame seeds, place seeds in a 6-ounce custard cup. Cook sesame seeds at High for 3 minutes till golden, stirring after 2 minutes, then after each minute.

Flaming

To flame a sauce for dessert, place 2 to 4 tablespoons brandy or rum in a 2-cup measuring cup. Heat at High for 15 to 20 seconds. Carefully ignite with a long match and pour over dessert.

25

Reheating

The microwave oven reheats most foods without loss of flavor or texture. Whether you make a dish in advance or are serving leftovers, the food will be fresh-tasting. Most foods are reheated from a refrigerated state. If you prepare food an hour or two before serving time and let it stand at room temperature, reduce the reheating time. Stir or rotate food as you would during cooking.

Reheating renews flavor

Dad's stuck in a traffic jam, Junior is still at his guitar lesson, Mom's working late—some days it's just impossible to eat together. At times like this, your microwave oven can be your short-order cook. Simply plan to cook as usual, separating out the single portion for the latecomer. Then cover and refrigerate. Dad, Junior, or Mom can reheat that portion when they arrive. Or maybe it's just you for lunch, and you'd like to heat up what's left of last night's dinner. Put single servings on a plate and reheat quickly in the microwave oven. The flavor can be more like "just cooked" than foods reheated conventionally.

Another plus... you can go ahead with the kitchen clean-up at the normal time and only have a few dinner plates and utensils to care for later in the evening.

Crisp foods

Fried chicken is one example of a crisp food easily reheated in the microwave oven. Place a piece of white paper toweling under the chicken piece to absorb moisture. Microwave a 4-ounce piece of chicken at Medium High or Cook Power 7 (70%) for 2 minutes.

Using the probe

If your microwave oven comes with the temperature probe, you can reheat food to the proper temperature, always confident the microwave oven will shut off automatically. Heat casseroles to 165° (probe temperature setting 8). Remember to stir casseroles from the outside in to distribute heat and save time.

Dessert

Renew that fresh-from-the-oven flavor of home-baked pie in seconds. A wedge of pie takes only 30 seconds at Medium High or Cook Power 7 (70%). If you like, slices of cheese may be added the last 10 seconds to soften.

Plate meals

For a quick lunch or light supper, place 1½ cups soup or stew in 16-ounce bowl or dish and place on dinner plate. Cover with waxed paper and heat for 2 minutes 30 seconds at Medium High or Cook Power 7 (70%). Add choice of bread and heat for 20 seconds more or till hot.

Plate meals

In a matter of minutes you can enjoy a hot meal without dinner tasting like leftovers. Arrange thick or dense foods to the outside of the plate, with more delicate or easy-to-heat foods to the center. Remember to cover the plate meal with waxed paper. At Medium High or Cook Power 7 (70%) it will take about 2 minutes 30 seconds to 3 minutes to reheat your plate meal.

Meat and gravy

You can also reheat leftover slices of meat for another hot dinner meal. Add a sauce this time, or spoon on the leftover gravy, to keep the meat moist. And remember to cover the dish tightly to keep moisture in; reheat at Medium High or Cook Power 7 (70%).

Freezing

It's good to know that the "extras" from your family's favorite casserole or the raw foods from the supermarket can be frozen, defrosted fast, and cooked in the microwave. But there are a few simple guidelines to follow; let us show you how.

Freezer tips

Many home-cooked or partially-cooked food mixtures can be frozen successfully. Season foods lightly because some flavors intensify during freezing.

Remember that some foods don't freeze well because of flavor and texture changes. These include fried foods, boiled dessert frostings, hard-cooked egg whites, green onions, radishes, cucumbers, and salad greens. Mayonnaise and sour cream may separate.

Containers

It's important to select moisture-vaporproof materials and containers for freezing. Check the packaging material first before defrosting, and especially before cooking, in the microwave. Look for labels telling you it is microwave-safe. Plastic pouches and freezer-weight plastic bags can go directly from freezer to microwave. But remember to slit the bag or tie it loosely to allow for the escape of steam.

Leave headspace

Allow headspace of about 2 inches between liquid foods and the top of the container. Wrap solid items tightly to remove as much air as possible.

Portions

Divide food into individual-size or family-size portions. Package in non-foil containers for microwave thawing and cooking. Food may also be transferred to a glass serving dish for heating after defrosting.

Save space

To save freezer space and reuse dishes, line casseroles, dishes, or plates with foil, plastic wrap, or freezer paper, leaving long ends. Fill, seal, and place container in the freezer. When the food is frozen, remove from the container; wrap, seal, label, and return to freezer.

Proper wrapping

Choose a moisture-vaporproof wrap designed specifically for freezing. Place food in the center of wrapping material. Bring the edges of the wrap together over the food. Fold the paper down in folds about 1 inch deep, pressing the wrap closely to the food to force out air.

Freezer dinners

Make your own TV dinners with paper plates and leftovers. Start with partitioned plates specifically designed for microwave oven use. Add single portions of cooked foods such as meat, gravy, and vegetables. Wrap singly in freezer paper or a plastic freezer bag; label.

Freeze 3 to 4 weeks. To heat, leave the plate in the freezer wrap. Cook at High for 6 to 7 minutes. Slide the paper plate onto a dinner plate; unwrap to serve. Increase the cooking time if you freeze larger portions.

Next, push out air as you make creases at the ends into points. Double-fold the ends up snugly to the center of the package to seal out air. Seal with freezer tape and label with contents, number of servings, and the date the food was frozen.

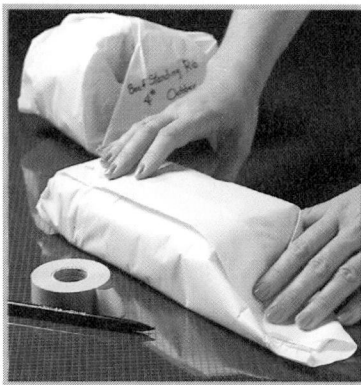

29

Defrosting

The chart on pages 32-34 is a general thawing guide. Since the shape of the frozen package or meat cut, the package weight, and the starting temperature may vary from the chart, expect the times shown to be close, but not necessarily exact. Timings are for foods frozen in a chest or upright freezer.

How to defrost

1. Check the packaging material first. Freezer paper, commercial plastic pouches, and freezer-weight plastic bags can go directly from the freezer to the microwave oven. Plastic packaging used for *refrigerated* storage of meats, poultry, and fish is heat sensitive and should be removed before defrosting. Foil or metal covers must be removed.

2. Leave properly packaged frozen foods in the original unopened package. Remove metal rings, clips, or paper-covered metal wires. On poultry, remove the metal ring that closes the bag; the large metal clip that holds the legs together may be left in place during defrosting.

3. Use defrosting directions on pages 32-34. *Times at Defrost* will usually yield partially thawed foods rather than completely thawed. Food should be cool to the touch; edges should be uncooked or very slightly cooked and the center icy. Test foods by pushing a fork into the center; if difficult to pierce, add defrosting time. Complete the defrosting process by allowing the recommended standing time. Foods should yield to moderate fork pressure. Foods should be completely thawed before cooking.

4. Never leave thawed food at room temperature longer than the suggested standing time. Refrigerate food that is not cooked immediately. Never refreeze thawed uncooked food.

Rotate the dish

Foods that cannot be stirred, rearranged, or turned over during defrosting (such as lasagna) should be rotated. Give the dish a quarter turn or half turn halfway through the defrosting time.

Flex the pouch

Plastic pouches can go directly from the freezer to microwave oven. Flex the pouch several times during the defrosting time to break up the food and allow the heat to be distributed evenly.

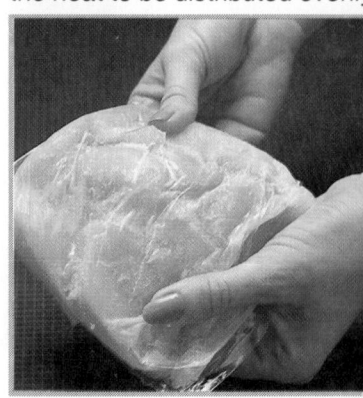

Shield uneven areas

Even-shaped round foods defrost and cook most evenly. The edges of uneven-shaped foods like meat, poultry, or recipes prepared in square and rectangular dishes, may defrost faster than the center. Use small pieces of foil to shield the food from excessive microwave energy. Don't let the foil touch the sides of the microwave oven.

Covering

Place unwrapped foods or packaged foods which may have juices in a casserole or baking dish. Cover unwrapped foods loosely with waxed paper to trap and distribute the heat evenly. Pierce the plastic packaging on poultry to allow for the escape of steam. Stir casseroles from the outside in, turn the dish, or rearrange foods as necessary.

Turn pieces

Some foods such as steaks, chops, and poultry pieces should be turned and rearranged during defrosting to help thaw evenly. Some items must be turned more than others.

1-step defrost-cook

When defrosting ground meat to shape into patties, loaves, or meatballs, it is important to use the Defrost setting for even thawing. (See pages 32-34 for specific times.) However, if you plan to continue cooking the ground meat before adding it to a recipe (such as a casserole, meat filling, or soup), you can defrost the meat at High. Use a glass mixing bowl or baking dish. Stir and break up the meat as it cooks. Spoon off the excess fat.

DEFROSTING CHART

FOOD	AMOUNT (Weight, Size)	QUICK DEFROST	STANDARD DEFROST Medium Low, Cook Power 3 (30%)
Beef Roasts Chuck Pot Roast	3 pounds (1½ to 2 inches thick)	Set **Quick Defrost** for 12:00 minutes. After 6:00 minutes of defrosting, turn the pot roast over. Let the roast stand for 5:00 minutes.	Cook at **Defrost** for 15 to 18 minutes, turning the roast over after 8 minutes of defrosting. Let stand for 5 minutes.
Boneless Rib Roast, rolled and tied	4 pounds (4-inch diameter)	Shield edges of roast with foil. Set **Quick Defrost** for 10:00 minutes. Let roast stand for 5:00 minutes. Turn roast over. Shield warm spots. Set **Quick Defrost** for 10:00 minutes. Let stand for 20:00 minutes.	Shield edges of roast with foil. Cook at **Defrost** for 34 to 38 minutes, turning roast over after 16 minutes of defrosting. Let stand for 10 minutes.
Beef Steaks Top Round Steak	1 pound (½ inch thick)	Set **Quick Defrost** for 4:00 minutes. Let stand for 5:00 minutes.	Cook at **Defrost** for 6 to 8 minutes. Let stand for 5 minutes.
Round Steak, whole	1½ pounds (½ inch thick)	Set **Quick Defrost** for 5:00 minutes. Let stand for 5:00 minutes.	Cook at **Defrost** for 8 to 9 minutes. Let stand for 5 minutes.
T-Bone Steak	1 pound (¾ inch thick)	Set **Quick Defrost** for 4:00 minutes. Let stand for 5:00 minutes.	Cook at **Defrost** for 5 to 6 minutes. Let stand for 5 minutes.
Sirloin Steak	2 pounds (1 inch thick)	Set **Quick Defrost** for 8:00 minutes. Let stand for 5:00 minutes.	Cook at **Defrost** for 11 to 12 minutes. Let stand for 5 minutes.
Other Beef Stew Meat	1 pound (1-inch cubes)	Set **Quick Defrost** for 4:30 minutes. After 3:00 minutes of defrosting, separate the meat pieces. Let meat stand for 5:00 minutes.	Cook at **Defrost** for 8 to 9 minutes, separating the meat pieces after 5 minutes of defrosting. Let stand for 5 minutes before using.
Ground Beef	1 pound	Set **Quick Defrost** for 5:00 minutes. After 2:30 minutes of defrosting, turn the ground beef over. Let meat stand for 5:00 minutes.	Cook at **Defrost** for 8 to 8½ minutes, turning the ground beef over after 4 minutes of defrosting. Let ground beef stand for 5 minutes.
	2 pounds	Set **Quick Defrost** for 9:00 minutes. After 4:30 minutes of defrosting, turn the ground beef over. Let meat stand for 5:00 minutes.	Cook at **Defrost** for 16 to 18 minutes, turning meat over after 10 minutes of defrosting. Let stand for 5 minutes.
Ground Beef 1-Step Defrost and Cook	1 pound	Set **High** for 8:30 minutes. After 5:00 minutes of cooking, break up the meat. Continue cooking, stirring the meat 3 times. Drain off the excess fat before adding additional ingredients as specific recipe directs.	Cook at **High** for 5 minutes. Break up the meat. Continue cooking at **High** for 3½ minutes, stirring 3 times. Drain off the excess fat before adding additional ingredients as specific recipe directs.
Ground Beef Patties	4 (4 ounces each)	Set **Quick Defrost** for 3:00 minutes. After 2:00 minutes of defrosting, give dish a half turn. Let stand for 5:00 minutes.	Cook at **Defrost** for 6 to 7 minutes, turning the meat patties over and giving the dish a half turn after 4 minutes of defrosting. Let stand for 5 minutes.

DEFROSTING CHART

FOOD	AMOUNT (Weight, Size)	QUICK DEFROST	STANDARD DEFROST Medium Low, Cook Power 3 (30%)
Chicken* Broiler-Fryer, whole	2½ to 3 pounds	Place poultry breast down. Set **Quick Defrost** for 12:00 minutes. After 6:00 minutes of defrosting, turn breast up. Place in bowl of cool water for 10:00 minutes; remove giblets before using.	Cook, breast down, at **Defrost** for 10 minutes. Cook, breast up, at **Defrost** for 10 minutes. Place in a bowl of cool water for 10 minutes; remove giblets before using.
Broiler-Fryer, cut up	2½ to 3 pounds	Set **Quick Defrost** for 11:00 minutes. After 5:30 minutes of defrosting, separate the chicken pieces. Let stand for 5:00 minutes.	Cook at **Defrost** for 18 to 20 minutes, separating the chicken pieces after 12 minutes. Let stand for 5 minutes.
Breasts	1½ to 2 pounds (2 whole)	Set **Quick Defrost** for 7:00 minutes, turning once. Separate the chicken pieces before standing time. Let stand for 5:00 minutes.	Cook at **Defrost** for 8 to 10 minutes, turning once. Separate the chicken pieces before standing time. Let stand for 5 minutes.
Cornish Hens*	1 (1¼ pounds)	Place poultry breast down. Set **Quick Defrost** for 6:00 minutes. After 3:00 minutes of defrosting, turn hen breast up. Place hen in bowl of cool water for 10:00 to 15:00 minutes; remove the giblets before using.	Cook, breast down, at **Defrost** for 6 minutes. Turn breast up. Cook at **Defrost** for 5 to 6 minutes. Place in bowl of cool water for 10 to 15 minutes; remove giblets before using.
	2 (1¼ pounds each)	Place hens breast down. Set **Quick Defrost** for 10:00 minutes. After 5:00 minutes of defrosting, turn hens breast up. Place in bowl of cool water for 10:00 to 15:00 minutes; remove the giblets before using.	Cook, breast down, at **Defrost** for 9 minutes. Turn breast up. Cook at **Defrost** for 8 to 9 minutes. Place in bowl of cool water for 10 to 15 minutes; remove giblets before using.
Duckling* Whole	5 pounds	Remove duckling from package; place breast down. Set **Quick Defrost** for 20:00 minutes. After 10:00 minutes of defrosting, turn breast up. Run cool water into cavity till giblets can be removed. Let duckling stand for 10:00 minutes before using.	Remove duckling from package; place breast down. Cook at **Defrost** for 12 minutes. Cook, breast up, at **Defrost** for 12 minutes. Let stand for 10 minutes. Cook, breast up, at **Defrost** for 10 minutes. Run cool water into cavity till giblets can be removed. Let duckling stand for 10 minutes before using.
Turkey* Boneless Turkey Roast	3 pounds	Remove from foil pan; place in baking dish. Set **Quick Defrost** for 18:00 minutes. After 9:00 minutes of defrosting turn roast over; shield warm areas with foil. Let stand for 30:00 minutes.	Remove from foil pan; place in baking dish. Cook at **Defrost** for 25 to 30 minutes. After 15 minutes of defrosting, turn turkey roast over; shield warm areas with foil. Let stand for 30 minutes.
Turkey Breast	5 to 6 pounds	Remove turkey from package. Set **Quick Defrost** for 6:00 minutes per pound. After ½ of defrosting time, turn over. Shield warm areas with foil after turning. Let stand for 10:00 minutes.	Remove turkey from package. Cook at **Defrost** for 10 minutes per pound. Turn over once. After turning, shield warm areas of turkey breats with foil. Let stand for 10 minutes.

*Poultry must be completely defrosted before cooking.

DEFROSTING CHART

FOOD	AMOUNT (Weight, Size)	QUICK DEFROST	STANDARD DEFROST Medium Low, Cook Power 3 (30%)
Turkey* Whole	Up to 14 pounds	Remove packaging. Cover wing tips with foil; uncover tips after ½ of the defrosting time. Set **Quick Defrost** for 5:00 minutes per pound, rotating bird after each ⅓ of the defrosting time and letting stand 10 minutes each time bird is rotated. (Cover parts that begin to brown with foil.) Let turkey stand for 30:00 minutes. Remove the giblets and neck. If ice crystals remain, rinse cavity with cold water and drain thoroughly. Cook turkey the same day.	Remove packaging. Cook at **Defrost** for 10 minutes per pound. Rotate bird a quarter turn after every 30 minutes of defrosting time, letting stand 5 minutes each time bird is rotated. (Cover parts that begin to brown with foil.) Let turkey stand about 30 minutes. Remove the giblets and neck. If ice crystals remain, rinse cavity with cold water and drain thoroughly. Cook turkey the same day.
Fish and Seafood Fish Fillets	1-pound block	Leave fish in packaging. Set **Quick Defrost** for 4:30 minutes, turning fish over after ½ of the defrosting time. Separate fillets before standing time, if possible. Let fish stand for 5:00 minutes. (Some fish varieties require up to 20:00 minutes total standing time to separate.)	Leave fish in packaging. Cook at **Defrost** for 7 minutes, turning fish over after ½ of the defrosting time. Separate fillets before standing time, if possible. Let stand for 5 minutes. (Some fish varieties require up to 20 minutes total standing time to separate.)
Lobster Tails	1 (8 ounces)	Set **Quick Defrost** for 2:30 minutes.	Cook at **Defrost** for 5 minutes. Let stand for 5 minutes.
Shrimp	1 pound	Set **Quick Defrost** for 4:30 minutes.	Cook at **Defrost** for 5 to 7 minutes. Let stand for 5 minutes.
Pork* Boneless Loin Roast, rolled and tied	4 pounds	Shield edges with foil. Set **Quick Defrost** for 14:00 minutes. Let stand for 5:00 minutes. Turn roast over. Shield any warm areas with foil. Set **Quick Defrost** for 10:00 minutes. Let stand for 20:00 minutes.	Shield edges with foil. Cook at **Defrost** for 22 to 26 minutes. After 12 minutes of defrosting, turn roast over. Let stand for 20 minutes.
Pork Chops	4 (4 ounces each)	Set **Quick Defrost** for 4:00 minutes. After 2:00 minutes of defrosting, separate the pieces.	Cook at **Defrost** for 6 to 7 minutes. After 4 minutes of defrosting, separate the pieces. Let stand for 5 minutes.
Spareribs	2 pounds	Set **Quick Defrost** for 6:30 minutes. After 3:15 minutes of defrosting, turn meat over and separate the pieces. Let stand for 5:00 minutes.	Cook at **Defrost** for 12 minutes. After 6 minutes of defrosting, turn meat over and separate the pieces. Let stand for 5 minutes before using.
Bacon	1-pound package	Leave bacon in the packaging. Set **Quick Defrost** for 2:00 minutes. Defrost just till slices separate.	Leave bacon in the packaging. Cook at **Defrost** for 3 to 3½ minutes, just till slices separate. Let stand for 5 minutes.
Frankfurters	1-pound package	Leave frankfurters in packaging. Set **Quick Defrost** for 2:30 minutes, turning package over once.	Leave frankfurters in packaging. Cook at **Defrost** for 4 minutes, turning package over once.
Frozen Fruit	10-ounce carton	Remove one metal carton end if present. Set **Quick Defrost** for 2:00 minutes. Defrost till thawed.	Remove one metal carton end if present. Cook at **Defrost** for 3 to 4 minutes or till thawed.

*Poultry and pork must be completely defrosted before cooking.

Meats & Main Dishes

No matter how demanding your schedule is, your microwave oven is guaranteed to make meal preparation faster and easier. This chapter is brimming with a variety of main-dish recipes. From a hearty ground beef casserole to a family-favorite Sunday roast, you'll find just what you need to build a menu around.

The techniques for cooking meat will vary according to the size, shape, composition, and tenderness of the meat cut. Specific techniques and details are included by section throughout this chapter.

Browning ground beef

It's handy to brown ground beef with chopped onion, green pepper, or other vegetables for use in sandwiches, chili, and casseroles. In a large bowl combine 1 pound ground beef and ½ cup of chopped vegetables. Cook, uncovered, at High for 5 minutes, stirring 3 times. Drain off excess fat and continue with your favorite recipe.

If your ground meat recipe contains pork, additional cooking time may be required for thorough cooking doneness of pork.

Wrappings & defrosting

Whether you purchase food in a refrigerated state and freeze at home or you purchase it already frozen, check the packaging material *before* freezing, as well as *before* defrosting.

Plastic packaging used for the refrigerated storage of meats is not adequate for freezer storage. Overwrap these packages with moisture-vaporproof freezer paper, foil, or plastic freezer bags to freeze; remove before defrosting. Plastic packaging used for refrigerated storage is heat sensitive and must be removed before defrosting in the microwave oven. (Sometimes the wrapping is creased and frozen into the meat or food, making it difficult to remove. Defrost the meat just till the wrapping is loosened; re-

move.) Foil or metal covers also must be removed from food before defrosting.

Leave properly packaged frozen foods in the original unopened package. Remove all metal rings, clips, or paper-covered metal wires. Freezer paper, freezer-weight plastic bags, and commercial plastic pouches can go directly from the freezer to the microwave oven for defrosting.

Defrosting ground meat

To defrost ground meat frozen in refrigerator plastic packaging, unwrap and place meat in a baking dish. Cover dish loosely with waxed paper. (If frozen in freezer-weight paper or microwave-safe plastic, it's safe to defrost in the packaging.)

After defrosting for the recommended time, pierce the meat in the center with a fork. If you can push the fork into the center of the meat using moderate pressure, the meat is ready for the suggested standing time. If it is difficult to pierce, it means a few more minutes of microwave defrosting time are needed.

Leftover burgers

Leftover burgers can make a return performance in any of the following delightful new guises:

Reheat one hamburger, without the bun, loosely covered, at Medium High or Cook Power 7 (70%) for 1 minute 15 seconds.

Garnish cooked hamburger patties with toppings such as guacamole, a dollop of sour cream dip, or a heap of sautéed fresh mushroom slices.

Sauce the meat patties with quick hollandaise from a package mix or creamy mushroom gravy from canned condensed cream soup.

Crumble the cooked meat into a bowl of chili, spaghetti sauce, or taco sauce.

Stir burger pieces into a simmering cheese soup or Oriental vegetable stir-fry.

Beef up the cheese filling for manicotti shells or a rice filling for stuffed green peppers.

Sprinkle well-seasoned hamburger chunks on a pizza or into corn bread batter.

Defrosting-cooking in 1 step

Defrost and cook ground meat in one easy step for use in a favorite casserole, soup or stew, or spaghetti sauce. First, unwrap and place the block of frozen ground meat in a bowl or baking dish. Defrost 1 pound of frozen meat, covered loosely with waxed paper, according to defrosting and cooking directions on page 32.

Next, break up the thawed ground meat with a fork. Continue cooking the meat as directed, breaking up the meat and stirring twice. Microwave cooking extracts more fat than conventional cooking of ground meat, so spoon off excess fat during cooking.

Spoon off and discard any remaining fat accumulated in the bottom of the bowl or dish. Use the cooked and crumbled meat in casseroles, omelets, pizzas, and other family-favorite recipes.

GROUND MEAT

LASAGNA

Total cooking time: 56 minutes

- 5 cups hot water
- 1 tablespoon cooking oil
- 9 uncooked lasagna noodles (about 8 ounces)
- 1 pound ground beef
- ¼ pound bulk pork sausage
- ½ cup chopped onion
- ¼ cup chopped green pepper
- 1 clove garlic, minced
- 1 16-ounce can tomatoes, cut up
- 1 12-ounce can tomato paste
- 1 teaspoon dried basil, crushed
- 1 teaspoon dried oregano, crushed
- 1 teaspoon brown sugar
- ¼ teaspoon pepper
- 1 cup ricotta cheese
- 2 eggs
- ½ cup grated Parmesan cheese
- 1 tablespoon dried parsley flakes
- ½ teaspoon dried basil, crushed
- 2 cups shredded mozzarella cheese

Combine water, oil, and ½ teaspoon *salt* in 12x7½x2-inch baking dish. Cover loosely with vented plastic wrap. Cook at **HIGH** for 10 minutes till boiling. Add noodles. Cook, covered, at **HIGH** for 10 minutes till noodles are tender but still firm, rotating dish a half turn after 5 minutes. Rinse noodles well under cool water; drain well. Combine ground beef, pork sausage, onion, green pepper, and garlic in a 2-quart casserole. Cook, uncovered, at **HIGH** for 6 minutes till meat is thoroughly done and is no longer pink, stirring to break up meat once. Add more cooking time, if necessary. Drain off fat. Stir in tomatoes, tomato paste, 1 teaspoon basil, oregano, brown sugar, pepper, and ½ teaspoon *salt*. Cover and cook at **MEDIUM HIGH or COOK POWER 7 (70%)** for 10 minutes till heated through. In a medium mixing bowl combine ricotta cheese, eggs, Parmesan, parsley flakes, and the ½ teaspoon basil. In 12x7½x2-inch baking dish, layer ⅓ each of the noodles, ricotta mixture, meat sauce, and the mozzarella. Repeat the layers twice, reserving last ⅓ mozzarella. Cover with waxed paper. Cook at **MEDIUM HIGH or COOK POWER 7 (70%)** for 20 minutes till hot. Sprinkle with remaining mozzarella. Let stand 10 minutes. Makes 8 servings.

BEEF AND PORK CHOW MEIN

Total cooking time: 14 minutes, 30 seconds

- ½ pound ground beef
- ½ pound ground pork
- 1 medium onion, sliced and separated into rings
- 1 medium green pepper, cut into thin strips
- 1 cup sliced celery
- ¼ cup soy sauce
- ¼ cup cornstarch
- 1 teaspoon instant beef bouillon granules
- ¼ teaspoon ground ginger
- 1 16-ounce can chow mein vegetables, drained
- 1 8-ounce can sliced water chestnuts, drained
- Warmed chow mein noodles

In 2-quart casserole combine meats, onion, green pepper, and celery. Cover; cook at **HIGH** for 7 minutes till sausage is thoroughly done and vegetables are crisp-tender, stirring twice. Add more cooking time, if necessary. Drain fat; set meat mixture aside. In 4-cup measure blend soy, cornstarch, bouillon, ginger, and 1½ cups *water*. Cook at **HIGH** for 4½ minutes till thickened, stirring after 2 minutes, then every minute. Add soy mixture, chow mein vegetables, and water chestnuts to meat. Cook at **HIGH** for 3 minutes till hot, stirring once. Serve over noodles. Serves 4.

LAYERED RAVIOLI CASSEROLE

Total cooking time: 10 minutes

- 1 pound ground beef
- 1 8-ounce can pizza sauce
- 1 15-ounce can spinach, well drained
- 1 cup cream-style cottage cheese with chives
- 1 15-ounce can ravioli in tomato sauce
- 3 tablespoons grated Parmesan cheese

In 1-quart casserole crumble ground beef. Cook at **HIGH** for 5 minutes, stirring 3 times. Drain fat. Stir in pizza sauce. In 10x6x2-inch baking dish spread spinach. Top with half the meat sauce, the cottage cheese, ravioli, and remaining meat sauce. Cook at **HIGH** for 5 minutes. Top with Parmesan. Makes 4 servings.

SPAGHETTI PIE

Total cooking time: 17 minutes

- 6 ounces spaghetti
- 1 pound ground beef
- ½ cup chopped onion
- ¼ cup chopped green pepper
- 1 7½-ounce can tomatoes, cut up
- 1 6-ounce can tomato paste
- 1 teaspoon sugar
- 1 teapoon dried oregano, crushed
- ½ teaspoon garlic salt
- 2 tablespoons butter or margarine
- ⅓ cup grated Parmesan cheese
- 2 beaten eggs
- 1 cup cream-style cottage cheese (8 ounces)
- ½ cup shredded mozzarella cheese

On top of range begin cooking spaghetti according to package directions. Meanwhile, in 1½-quart bowl crumble meat. Add onion and green pepper. Cook at **HIGH** for 5 minutes, stirring 3 times. Drain fat. Stir in undrained tomatoes, tomato paste, sugar, oregano, and garlic salt. Cover; cook at **HIGH** for 3 minutes, stirring once. Set aside. When the spaghetti is tender, drain. Stir in butter, Parmesan, and eggs. Form into a "crust" in 10-inch pie plate. Cook at **HIGH** for 2 minutes. Spread cottage cheese over bottom of "crust"; fill with tomato mixture. Cover; cook at **HIGH** for 6 minutes till hot, giving dish half turn after 3 minutes. Top with the mozzarella. Cook, uncovered, at **HIGH** for 1 minute till cheese melts. Let stand 8 to 10 minutes. Garnish with snipped parsley, if desired. Makes 6 servings.

HAM-PIZZA BURGERS

Total cooking time: 5 minutes

- ½ pound ground fully cooked ham
- ¾ cup shredded mozzarella cheese (3 ounces)
- ¼ cup chopped dill pickle
- ¼ cup finely chopped onion
- 2 tablespoons diced green pepper
- ½ cup canned pizza sauce
- 6 hamburger buns, split and toasted

In 1½-quart bowl mix all ingredients except buns. Cook at **HIGH** for 5 minutes till hot; stir once. Serve on buns. Serves 6.

Reheating

Use the microwave to warm small amounts of already cooked foods. The times below are for reheating from refrigerator storage temperature. Cover food and heat in microwave safe container at **MEDIUM HIGH or COOK POWER 7 (70%)**. Heat main dishes containing sour cream or cheese at **MEDIUM or COOK POWER 5 (50%)**.

FOOD	AMOUNT	TIME
Dinner:		
Meat, potato, and vegetable	1 serving each on dinner plate	2½ to 3 minutes
Meats:		
Chicken	4-ounce piece	2 minutes
Sliced beef, pork, ham, or turkey	2-ounce slice	1 to 1¼ minutes
Hamburger (without bun)	1 patty	1 minute
Pork chop	1	1½ minutes
Main Dishes:		
Meat-vegetable casserole	1 cup	3½ to 4 minutes
Chili	1 cup	3½ to 4 minutes
Spaghetti sauce	1 cup	4 minutes
Beef Stew	1 cup	3½ to 4 minutes

Meat loaf pointers

There is a secret to success in making a tender, juicy meat loaf. And you'll learn how easy it really is! First, mix the egg, liquid, crumbs, and seasoning ingredients together in a bowl. Then crumble in the ground meat. Mix lightly till it is well combined. Overmixing will result in a compact loaf. When shaping the loaf, handle the meat mixture only as much as necessary.

Shaping into ring

A basic meat loaf mixture can be shaped in several different ways. To make a ring shape, press the meat mixture into a glass or plastic ring mold baking dish (or position a custard cup, right side up, in center of a round baking dish) or form meat mixture into a ring shape in an 8x8x2-inch baking dish. Cover with waxed paper; micro-cook according to the specific recipe directions.

All meat loaves should be thoroughly cooked to an internal temperature of 170°F till no longer pink. Test meat in 3 areas with a meat thermometer. Add more cooking time, if necessary. Do not prepare meat loaves in the microwave oven if the recipe calls for ground pork; substitute ground beef, turkey, or lamb.

Shaping into oval

Shape the meat mixture into an oval shape for faster and more even microwave cooking than the traditional loaf shape.

To make an oval-shaped loaf, press the meat mixture into a 1½-quart oval baking dish. (Or, shape mixture into an oval shape in 8x8x2-inch or 10x6x2-inch baking dish.) Cover with waxed paper and micro-cook as the recipe directs.

Individual loaves

To make individual meat loaves, divide the meat mixture into equal portions. Mold into even-shaped loaves. Arrange loaves in a 12x7½x2-inch baking dish. Cover with waxed paper; micro-cook as recipe directs.

LOAVES

ROLLED STUFFED MEAT LOAF

Total cooking time: 29 minutes

- 2 eggs, slightly beaten
- ⅓ cup fine dry bread crumbs
- ¼ cup milk
- 1 teaspoon onion powder
- ½ teaspoon dry mustard
- 1½ pounds ground beef
- ⅓ cup chopped carrot
- ⅓ cup chopped celery
- 2 tablespoons butter or margarine
- 1 cup herb-seasoned stuffing croutons, crushed
- 1 2-ounce can mushroom stems and pieces, drained

In bowl combine first 5 ingredients and 1 teaspoon *salt*. Add beef; mix well. On waxed paper, pat into a 12x8-inch rectangle. In small bowl combine carrot, celery, and butter. Cook at **HIGH** for 4 minutes till vegetables are tender. Stir in croutons, mushrooms, and ¼ cup *water*. Spoon down center of meat. Fold sides of meat over to center; seal seam and ends. Place meat roll, seam side down, in 12x7½x2-inch baking dish. Cook, covered, at **HIGH** for 5 minutes. Give dish a half turn. Cook, uncovered, at **MEDIUM HIGH or COOK POWER 7 (70%)** for 15 minutes. Add more cooking time, if necessary, till internal temperature of meat reaches 170°F when tested in 3 areas and meat is thoroughly cooked and no longer pink. Let stand 5 minutes. Makes 6 servings.

SPICY MEAT LOAVES

Total cooking time: 21 minutes

- 2 beaten eggs
- ¾ cup milk
- ⅔ cup fine dry bread crumbs
- 2 tablespoons finely chopped onion
- 1 teaspoon salt
- ½ teaspoon chili powder
  Dash pepper
- 1½ pounds ground beef
- ¼ cup hot-style catsup
- 1 tablespoon brown sugar
- ½ teaspoon dry mustard

In mixing bowl combine eggs, milk, bread crumbs, onion, salt, chili powder, and pepper. Add beef; mix well. Shape meat mixture into 6 individual loaves. Arrange the loaves in a 12x7½x2-inch baking dish. Cover; cook at **MEDIUM HIGH or COOK POWER 7 (70%)** for 14 minutes, rearranging loaves once. Drain fat. In bowl combine catsup, brown sugar, and dry mustard; spread atop loaves. Cook, uncovered, at **MEDIUM HIGH or COOK POWER 7 (70%)** for 2 minutes. Add more cooking time, if necessary, till internal temperature reaches 170°F when loaves are tested and meat is thoroughly cooked and no longer pink (juices should run clear). Let stand 5 minutes before serving. Serves 6.

Ring Loaf: Shape meat into ring in an 8-inch round baking dish. Cover; cook at **MEDIUM HIGH or COOK POWER 7 (70%)** for 12 to 14 minutes, giving dish a half turn once. Drain, glaze, and let stand as directed above.

STROGANOFF MEAT RING

Total cooking time: 11 minutes

- ½ of 10¾-ounce can (⅔ cup) condensed golden mushroom soup
- ⅓ cup dairy sour cream
- 1 beaten egg
- 1½ cups soft bread crumbs (2 slices bread)
- ¼ cup wheat germ
- ¼ teaspoon dried basil, crushed
  Dash pepper
  Dash garlic salt
- 1 pound lean ground beef
- 1 tablespoon dry white wine

Combine ¼ cup of the soup, ¼ cup of the sour cream, the egg, crumbs, wheat germ, and seasonings. Let stand 5 minutes. Add beef; mix well. In a 9-inch pie plate shape into ring. (If desired, place 6-ounce custard cup, right side up, in center of pie plate and mold mixture around cup.) Cover with waxed paper. Cook at **HIGH** for 9 minutes, giving plate half turn twice. Add more cooking time, if necessary, till internal temperature reaches 170°F when tested in 3 areas and meat is thoroughly cooked and no longer pink. Let stand 5 minutes. (Remove cup.) Drain juices. For sauce, in 2-cup measure or serving bowl stir together remaining soup, remaining sour cream, and the wine. Cook at **HIGH** for 2 minutes till hot. Pass sauce with meat. Serves 4.

41

Tips & Techniques

Cooking patties

Shape 1 pound of ground meat into 4 patties, about 4 inches in diameter. Place the patties in an 8x8x2-inch baking dish. Cook, covered with waxed paper, at High for 5 to 6 minutes.

Give the dish a half turn once about halfway through cooking time for more even cooking. Two patties may be prepared and cooked in the same manner for 3 minutes 30 seconds to 4 minutes, giving dish a half turn once.

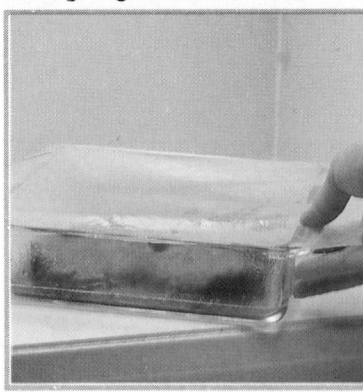

Do not prepare meat patties in the microwave oven if the recipe calls for ground pork; substitute ground beef, turkey, lamb, or veal. Cook till thoroughly cooked and no longer pink. Add more cooking time, if necessary.

Freezing patties

Shape the meat mixture into 4 even-sized patties. Freeze patties between pieces of waxed paper; tightly wrap. When ready to defrost, separate the patties and place in an 8x8x2-inch baking dish.

Defrosting patties

Next, defrost the meat patties, uncovered, according to defrosting directions on page 32, giving dish a half turn once. Remove any patties that are thawed.

Test for thawing doneness by piercing the patties in the center with a long-tined meat fork. If you can push the fork into the meat easily, it is thawed. Continue defrosting as directed above till meat patties are defrosted.

Freezer burgers

Keep some frozen hamburger patties on hand for quick sandwiches. Form ground chuck into patties 4 inches in diameter. Stack patties with double thicknesses of waxed paper between burgers. Place in freezer bags or wrap. Seal, label, and freeze. When ready to use, defrost and cook in the microwave.

BASIC BURGERS

Total cooking time: 5 minutes

> 1 pound ground chuck

Shape meat into 4 patties about 4 inches in diameter each. Place in 8x8x2-inch baking dish. Cover; cook patties at **HIGH** for 5 to 6 minutes, giving dish half turn once. Makes 4.

For 2 patties: Cook as above at **HIGH** for 3½ to 4 minutes.

Four patties in 10-inch browning dish: Preheat browning dish, uncovered, at **HIGH** for 5 minutes. Cook patties, covered, at **HIGH** for 2 minutes. Turn. Cook, covered, at **HIGH** for 1½ to 2 minutes.

Two patties in 10-inch browning dish: Preheat as above. Cook patties, covered, at **HIGH** for 1½ minutes. Turn; cook, covered, at **HIGH** for 1¼ to 1½ minutes more.

MEXICAN BURGERS

Total cooking time: 11 minutes

> 1 6-ounce container frozen avocado dip
> 1 tablespoon lemon juice
> Few drops bottled hot pepper sauce
> 1 small tomato, peeled, seeded, and chopped
> ½ cup crushed corn chips
> ⅓ cup milk
> 1 teaspoon Worcestershire sauce
> ½ teaspoon onion salt
> 1 pound ground beef
> 5 hamburger buns, split, toasted, and buttered

Remove the frozen avocado dip from container; place in small bowl. Cook at **MEDIUM LOW or COOK POWER 3 (30%)** for 5 minutes. Add lemon juice, hot pepper sauce, and tomato. In another bowl combine the corn chips, milk, Worcestershire, and onion salt; mix well. Add ground beef; mix well. Shape into 5 patties about 4 inches in diameter each. Place in a 12x7½x2-inch baking dish. Cover; cook at **HIGH** for 4 minutes. Rearrange and turn patties over; spoon off juices. Cover; cook at **HIGH** for 2 minutes. Serve burgers on toasted buns topped with avocado mixture. Makes 5 servings.

HERBED STUFFING BURGERS

Total cooking time: 13 minutes

> 1 cup herb-seasoned stuffing mix
> ¾ cup milk
> 1 teaspoon minced dried onion
> 1 pound ground beef
> ½ teaspoon salt
> ¼ teaspoon pepper
> 4 hamburger buns, split and toasted
> Onion rings
> Sliced tomatoes

Preheat 10-inch browning dish at **HIGH** for 5 minutes. Meanwhile, combine stuffing mix, milk, and onion; let stand till moistened. Add ground beef, salt, and pepper to stuffing mixture; mix well. Shape into 4 patties about 4 inches in diameter each. Cook in browning dish at **HIGH** for 4 minutes. Turn patties over. Continue cooking at **HIGH** for 3 minutes till done. Serve in buns topped with onion and tomatoes. Serves 4.

RELISH BURGERS

Total cooking time: 4 minutes

> 2 tablespoons cider vinegar
> 1 tablespoon sugar
> ½ teaspoon salt
> ⅛ teaspoon pepper
> ½ cup chopped onion
> ½ cup chopped tomato
> ½ cup cucumber cut into paper-thin slices
> 1 pound ground beef
> ¾ teaspoon salt
> Dash pepper
> 2 tablespoons chopped sweet pickle
> 4 hamburger buns, split

In bowl combine vinegar, sugar, the ½ teaspoon salt, and the ⅛ teaspoon pepper; add onion, tomato, and cucumber. Cover and refrigerate 1 to 2 hours; drain well. Combine beef and remaining salt and pepper; shape into 4 patties about 4 inches in diameter each. Place in an 8x8x2-inch baking dish. Cover and cook at **HIGH** for 5 minutes, giving dish half turn once. Stir chopped pickle into cucumber mixture. Serve burgers on buns topped with the cucumber relish. Makes 4 servings.

PATTIES

SAUERBRATEN BURGERS

Total cooking time: 13 minutes, 30 seconds

- 6 gingersnaps
- 1 8-ounce can tomato sauce
- ¼ cup finely chopped onion
- 2 tablespoons raisins
- ½ teaspoon salt
- 1 pound ground beef
- 3 tablespoons water
- 2 tablespoons vinegar
- 1 tablespoon brown sugar
- 1 teaspoon prepared mustard
  Dash pepper

Crush the gingersnaps with a rolling pin and reserve 2 tablespoons. In bowl combine remaining gingersnaps, ¼ cup of the tomato sauce, the onion, raisins, and salt. Add ground beef and mix well. Shape into 6 patties about 4 inches in diameter each. Place in 12x7½x2-inch baking dish. Cover and cook at **HIGH** for 6 minutes. Spoon off juices. Turn over and rearrange. Cover and cook at **HIGH** for 4 minutes more. In a small bowl combine the remaining tomato sauce, water, vinegar, brown sugar, mustard, and pepper. Pour over the burgers. Cover and cook at **HIGH** for 2 minutes. Remove burgers to platter and keep warm. Pour sauce into small bowl or heatproof pitcher. Stir in the reserved gingersnap crumbs. Cook, uncovered, at **HIGH** for 1½ minutes, stirring once. Pass the sauce with burgers. Makes 4 servings.

LAMB PATTIES WITH DILL SAUCE

Total cooking time: 11 minutes

- 1 beaten egg
- ¼ cup rolled oats
- ¼ cup chopped onion
- 1 teaspoon salt
  Dash pepper
- 1½ pounds ground lamb
- 1 tablespoon chopped onion
- 1 tablespoon butter or margarine
- 2 tablespoons all-purpose flour
- ½ teaspoon dried dillweed
- ½ teaspoon paprika
- ⅛ teaspoon salt
- 1 cup milk
- 2 tablespoons grated Parmesan cheese

In bowl combine egg, oats, the ¼ cup onion, 1 teaspoon salt, and pepper. Add lamb; mix well. Shape into 6 patties about 4 inches in diameter each. Arrange patties in 12x7½x2-inch baking dish. Cover and cook at **HIGH** for 4 minutes, rotating dish after 2 minutes. Turn patties over and rearrange. Cook at **HIGH** for 3 minutes more. In 2-cup measure combine the 1 tablespoon onion and butter. Cook, uncovered, at **HIGH** for 1½ minutes till tender but not brown. Stir in flour, dillweed, paprika, and the ⅛ teaspoon salt. Add milk all at once. Cook, uncovered, at **HIGH** for 2½ minutes, stirring every 30 seconds till thickened and bubbly. Stir in Parmesan cheese. Spoon sauce over patties. Makes 6 servings.

SALISBURY STEAK

Total cooking time: 11 minutes, 30 seconds

- 1 beaten egg
- ¼ cup finely crushed saltine crackers
- 1 tablespoon Worcestershire sauce
- 1 pound ground beef
- 1 1-ounce envelope brown gravy mix
- 1 small onion, thinly sliced and separated into rings
- 1 3½-ounce can sliced mushrooms, drained
- 1 cup water
  English muffins, split, or bread, toasted (optional)

Combine the egg, crushed crackers, and Worcestershire sauce. Add meat; mix well. Shape into 4 patties about ½ inch thick each. Arrange patties in an 8x8x2-inch baking dish. Cover with waxed paper. Cook at **HIGH** for 4 minutes. Turn patties over; cook, covered, at **HIGH** for 3 minutes. Remove patties to a serving platter. Keep warm. Skim fat from drippings; add gravy mix, onions, and mushrooms to drippings in dish. Stir in water. Cook, uncovered, at **HIGH** for 4½ minutes till thickened and bubbly, stirring every minute. Serve atop English muffins or bread, if desired. Serve gravy over patties. Serves 4.

Salisbury Steak

Shaping meatballs

Form a seasoned meat mixture into 1-inch meatballs. To shape meatballs into uniform size for even cooking, pat the meat mixture into a 1-inch-thick square on a sheet of waxed paper. Cut into 1-inch cubes, as shown. With your hands, round each cube of meat mixture into a ball.

Freezing meatballs

For easier freezer storage, remove the cooked meatballs to a large, shallow baking pan; arrange so the meatballs are not touching. Place the filled pan in the freezer and freeze meatballs just till frozen.

Place desired number of the frozen meatballs in freezer-weight plastic bags or plastic pouches. Seal, label, and store in the freezer until ready to use in your favorite recipe.

Cooking meatballs

Arrange meatballs in a 9-inch pie plate. Cook, covered with waxed paper, at Medium or Cook Power 5 (50%) for 8 minutes. Turn meatballs and rearrange. Repeat till all are cooked, draining fat as needed. Do not prepare meatballs in microwave oven if recipe calls for ground pork; substitute ground beef, turkey, lamb, or veal. Cook till thoroughly cooked and no longer pink. Add more cooking time, if necessary.

BASIC MEATBALLS

Total cooking time: 32 minutes

- 3 eggs
- ½ cup milk
- 3 cups soft bread crumbs (4 slices)
- ½ cup finely chopped onion
- 2 teaspoons salt
- 3 pounds ground beef

In large bowl beat eggs. Stir in milk, crumbs, onion, and salt. Add meat and mix well. Chill. With wet hands, shape meat mixture into 72 meatballs. Arrange 18 balls in 9-inch pie plate. Cook at **MEDIUM or COOK POWER 5 (50%)** for 8 minutes, turning meatballs and rearranging twice. Repeat till all are cooked. Place cooked meatballs on baking pan and place in freezer just till frozen. Using 24 meatballs per package, place in moisture-vaporproof containers or bags. Seal, label, and freeze. Makes 3 freezer portions, 24 meatballs each.

MEATBALL SANDWICH

Total cooking time: 10 minutes

- ½ cup catsup
- ⅓ cup chili sauce
- ¼ cup water
- 2 tablespoons brown sugar
- 1 tablespoon Worcestershire sauce
- 1 tablespoon prepared mustard
- 1 teaspoon celery seed
- ¼ teaspoon salt
- ¼ teaspoon garlic powder
  Few drops bottled hot pepper sauce
- 3 thin slices lemon
- ⅓ recipe (24) frozen Basic Meatballs
- 8 hard rolls or frankfurter buns, split and toasted
- 1 onion, sliced and separated into rings

In casserole combine catsup, chili sauce, water, brown sugar, Worcestershire, mustard, celery seed, salt, garlic powder, hot pepper sauce, and lemon slices. Cook at **HIGH** for 3 minutes, stirring once. Stir in frozen meatballs. Cover with waxed paper and cook at **HIGH** for 7 minutes till meatballs are heated through, stirring once. Remove lemon slices. Serve meatballs and sauce on toasted rolls. Garnish with onion rings. Makes 8 servings.

SPAGHETTI AND MEATBALLS

Total cooking time: 23 minutes

- ½ cup chopped onion
- ½ cup chopped green pepper
- 2 tablespoons water
- 2 20-ounce jars Italian cooking sauce
- ⅓ recipe (24) frozen Basic Meatballs
- 1 clove garlic, minced
- 1 tablespoon sugar
- ½ teaspoon chili powder
  Hot cooked spaghetti
  Grated Parmesan cheese

In 2½- or 3-quart casserole combine onion, green pepper, and water. Cover and cook at **HIGH** for 3 minutes. (Do not drain.) Stir in cooking sauce, frozen meatballs, garlic, sugar, and chili powder. Cover and cook at **MEDIUM HIGH or COOK POWER 7 (70%)** for 20 minutes till sauce is hot and meatballs are heated through. Serve over hot spaghetti. Pass Parmesan cheese. Makes 6 to 8 servings.

STROGANOFF MEATBALLS

Total cooking time: 14 minutes

- 1 10¾-ounce can condensed cream of mushroom soup
- ¾ cup milk
- 1 tablespoon catsup
- ¼ teaspoon dried thyme, crushed
- ⅛ teaspoon garlic powder
- ⅓ recipe (24) frozen Basic Meatballs
- ½ cup dairy sour cream
  Hot cooked rice or noodles
  Snipped parsley

In a 2-quart casserole blend soup and milk. Stir in catsup, thyme, and garlic powder. Cook at **HIGH** for 5 minutes till heated through, stirring every 2 minutes. Add meatballs. Cover and cook at **HIGH** for 8 minutes till sauce is bubbly and meatballs are heated through, stirring twice to separate meatballs. Stir ¾ cup of hot mixture into sour cream; return to casserole. Cook at **MEDIUM HIGH or COOK POWER 7 (70%)** for 1 minute just till hot. Serve over hot cooked rice or noodles. Sprinkle with snipped parsley. Makes 6 servings.

Slicing meat

Partially freeze meats, such as round steak, to make slicing and cutting easier and pieces more uniform. Allow the meat to thaw completely before cooking.

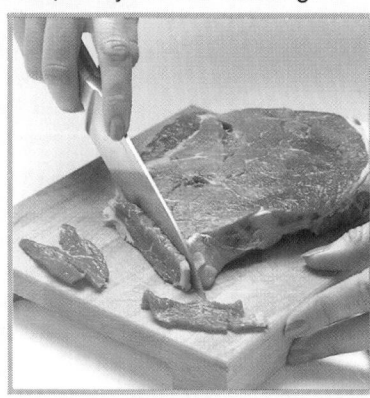

Cooking strips

Melt 2 tablespoons butter or margarine in 8x8x2-inch baking dish at High for 30 seconds. Add meat and seasonings. Cover; cook at High for 6 minutes or to desired doneness. Stir 3 times.

For pork, cook 1 pound pork strips, covered, for 10 minutes at Medium or Cook Power 5 (50%), stirring 3 times, till thoroughly done and no longer pink, adding more cooking time, if necessary.

Defrosting pieces

Place the unwrapped 1-pound package of frozen stew meat (about 1-inch cubes) in a baking dish. Cover dish loosely with waxed paper. (If the meat is pre-packaged in freezer paper, plastic pouches, or in freezer-weight plastic bags, it can be defrosted in the packaging, but slit or tie bag loosely to allow for the escape of steam.)

Defrost meat, covered with waxed paper, according to the defrosting directions on page 32, using a meat fork to separate and rearrange the meat pieces.

STRIPS & PIECES

PEPPER STEAK

Total cooking time: 39 minutes

- 1½ pounds beef round steak, cut ½ inch thick
- 1 7½-ounce can tomatoes, cut up
- ½ cup finely chopped onion
- 1 tablespoon instant beef bouillon granules
- 2 cloves garlic, minced
- 1 tablespoon Worcestershire sauce
- ¼ teaspoon pepper
- 2 medium green peppers, cut into strips
- ¼ cup all-purpose flour
  Hot cooked rice

Cut steak into thin bite-size strips. Place meat in a 2-quart casserole. Stir in tomatoes, onion, bouillon, garlic, Worcestershire, pepper, and 1¼ cups *water*. Cook, covered, at **MEDIUM HIGH or COOK POWER 7 (70%)** for 30 minutes till meat is tender, stirring once. Add green peppers. Combine flour and ⅓ cup *cold water;* stir into casserole. Cook, uncovered, at **HIGH** for 9 minutes till thickened and bubbly, stirring 3 times. Serve over hot rice. Serves 6.

BEEF TERIYAKI

Total cooking time: 5 minutes

- 1 pound boneless beef tenderloin or sirloin, cut 1 inch thick
- ½ cup soy sauce
- ¼ cup sake or dry sherry
- 4 cloves garlic, minced
- 2 tablespoons sugar
- 2 teaspoons dry mustard

Thinly slice beef across the grain into bite-size strips. (Partially frozen meat is easier to cut. Allow meat to thaw completely before cooking.) In bowl combine soy sauce, sake, garlic, sugar, and mustard. Add meat to soy mixture; let stand at room temperature for 15 minutes. Drain meat, reserving marinade. Thread, accordion style, on small bamboo skewers. Place skewers in a 12x7½x2-inch baking dish. Cook, uncovered, at **HIGH** for 5 minutes for medium or to desired doneness, brushing with reserved marinade and turning over skewers once. Makes 4 servings.

BEEF-ASPARAGUS ORIENTAL

Total cooking time: 11 minutes

- 1 pound beef flank steak
- 12 fresh asparagus spears
- 2 tablespoons soy sauce
- 1 tablespoon cornstarch
- 1 tablespoon cooking oil
- 1 teaspoon sugar
- 2 tablespoons dry white wine
- 2 tablespoons chicken broth
  Hot cooked rice

Thinly slice steak across grain. (Partially frozen meat is easier to cut. Allow meat to thaw completely before cooking.) Cut the asparagus diagonally into 1-inch pieces. In 1-quart casserole combine asparagus and ¼ cup *water*. Cover; cook at **HIGH** for 4 minutes, stirring once. Drain; set aside. Place meat in an 8x8x2-inch baking dish. Mix soy, cornstarch, oil, and sugar; pour over beef. Cover; cook at **HIGH** for 6 minutes till meat is cooked, stirring twice. Add asparagus, wine, and broth. Cook at **HIGH** for 1 minute, stirring once. Serve over rice. Makes 4 servings.

BEEF BURGUNDY

Total cooking time: 18 minutes, 30 seconds

- 1 pound boneless beef sirloin steak
- 2 cups sliced fresh mushrooms
- ½ cup chopped onion
- 1 clove garlic, crushed
- ¼ cup butter or margarine
- 1 tablespoon snipped parsley
- 1 bay leaf
- 1 cup burgundy
- ¾ cup cold water
- ¼ cup all-purpose flour
  Hot cooked rice

Cut steak into strips ¼ inch wide and 2 inches long. (Partially frozen meat is easier to cut. Allow meat to thaw completely before cooking.) In 3-quart casserole combine mushrooms, onion, garlic, and butter. Cover; cook at **HIGH** for 4 minutes. Add steak, parsley, bay leaf, ¾ teaspoon *salt,* and dash *pepper.* Stir in wine. Cover; cook at **HIGH** for 12 minutes, stirring once. Combine water and flour; stir into mixture. Cook at **HIGH** for 2½ minutes till bubbly, stirring once. Serve over rice. Serves 4.

49

Tips & Techniques

BACON & SAUSAGE

Arranging bacon strips

Place 2 sheets of paper toweling on a microwave-safe plate or place a microwave roasting rack in shallow baking dish. Arrange up to 8 slices of bacon on the paper toweling or rack. Cover with 2 sheets of paper toweling to prevent spattering. Replace paper toweling as necessary.

Cooking bacon on a rack

To cook bacon on microwave roasting rack, place slices on rack in baking dish. Cover bacon with 2 sheets of paper toweling to prevent spattering. Cook till crisp at High (refer to exact timings in chart on page 51).

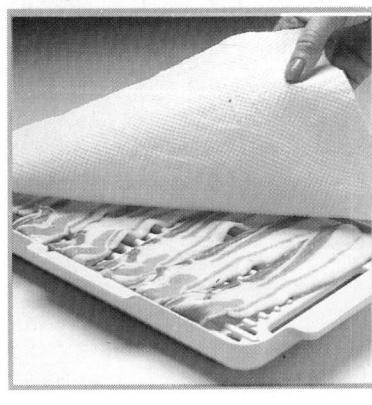

Cooking bacon on a plate

Cook bacon strips till crisp at High (refer to exact timings in chart on page 51). Cooking times will vary depending on the thickness of the slice. For bacon with drippings, omit paper toweling under bacon or cook the bacon slices, covered, on a microwave roasting rack in baking dish.

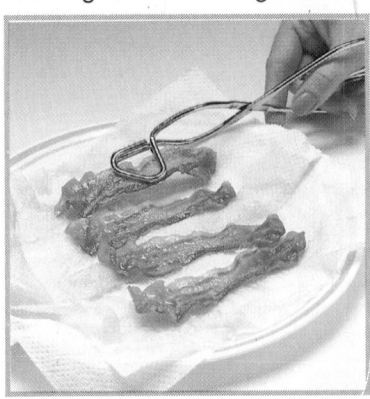

Defrosting bacon

Buy extra bacon when it's on special at the grocery store and freeze until ready to use (or repackage bacon in small units for specific uses).

To defrost, place wrapped 1-pound package bacon in a baking dish and defrost according to defrosting directions given on page 34, till the slices can be easily separated.

50

HOT POLISH POTATO SALAD

Total cooking time: 15 minutes, 30 seconds

- 2 **cups peeled and cubed potatoes (2 potatoes)**
- ¼ **cup water**
- 2 **slices bacon, halved**
- ¼ **cup chopped onion**
- 2 **tablespoons sugar**
- 1 **tablespoon all-purpose flour**
- ½ **teaspoon salt**
- ¼ **teaspoon celery seed**
  Dash pepper
- ¼ **cup water**
- 3 **tablespoons vinegar**
- 2 **fully cooked Polish sausages, cut into 1-inch pieces**
- 2 **tablespoons snipped parsley**

In a 1-quart casserole combine cubed potatoes and ¼ cup water. Cook at **HIGH** for 7 minutes. Drain in colander and set aside. In same casserole cook bacon, covered, at **HIGH** for 2 minutes. Remove bacon with slotted soon, reserving drippings in casserole. Crumble bacon and set aside. Add chopped onion to the reserved drippings. Cook, covered, at **HIGH** for 1½ minutes. Stir in sugar, flour, salt, celery seed, and pepper. Add ¼ cup water and vinegar; cook, uncovered, at **HIGH** for 1½ minutes or till mixture is thickened and bubbly, stirring once. Stir in potatoes and sausage. Cook, covered, at **HIGH** for 3½ minutes or till heated through, stirring once. Add more cooking time, if necessary. Sprinkle with parsley and bacon. Makes 2 servings.

Canadian-Style Bacon

Place ⅛- or ¼-inch-thick slices of Canadian-style bacon on dinner plate, platter, or in baking dish. Cover loosely with waxed paper and cook at HIGH till hot, rotating the dish once.

⅛-Inch-Thick Slices		¼-Inch-Thick Slices	
Number of Slices	Time at HIGH	Number of Slices	Time at HIGH
2	½ minute	2	1½ minutes
4	1 minute	4	2½ minutes
6	1½ minutes	6	3 minutes
8	2 minutes	8	4 minutes

Bacon

Arrange 1 to 8 slices on 2 layers of paper toweling on microwave-safe plate or in shallow baking dish. Or, arrange 1 to 8 slices on a microwave roasting rack in baking dish. Cover with 2 sheets of paper toweling to prevent spattering. (For bacon drippings, omit paper toweling under bacon or cook slices on a microwave roasting rack in baking dish.) Cook till crisp at HIGH for time on chart. Rearrange bacon when cooking 6 or 8 slices.

Number of Slices	Time at HIGH
2	2 to 2½ minutes
4	3½ to 4 minutes
6	5 to 6 minutes
8	6 to 7 minutes

Hot Dogs

Place hot dogs in buns and wrap each sandwich separately in a paper napkin. Heat at HIGH for time in chart.

Number of Hot Dogs	Time at HIGH
1	30 seconds
2	50 seconds
3	1 minute 20 seconds
4	1 minute 30 seconds
5	1 minute 50 seconds
6	2 minutes

Cutting round steak

Using a sharp knife, trim excess fat from the meat. Cut the meat in half. Or, cut meat into 4 serving-size portions for easier handling when freezing, defrosting, and cooking.

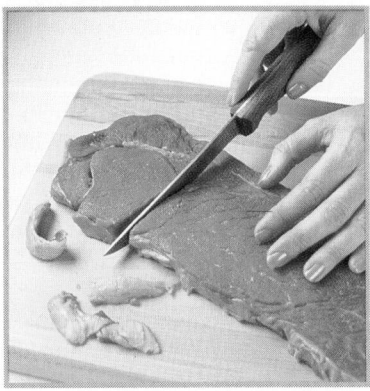

paper or freezer paper between each. The portions will separate easier and defrost faster.

Place the 4 frozen meat portions in a single layer in a 13x9x2-inch baking dish.

Pounding round steak

Place meat portions between 2 pieces of plastic wrap. Using a metal or wooden meat mallet, pound meat from center out to edges of meat. Pounding with the coarse-toothed edge of a mallet breaks some of the meat fibers and helps make the meat more tender.

Set Quick Defrost for 5 minutes. Turn dish after half the defrosting time. Let stand for 5 to 10 minutes. (Or, defrost the meat, covered with waxed paper, at Defrost or Cook Power 3 (30%) for 8 to 9 minutes, turning dish after 6 minutes. Let stand 5 to 10 minutes.) Test for thawing doneness by piercing center of meat with a fork. If meat yields to moderate pressure, it is ready for standing time. If difficult to pierce, add more defrosting time.

Defrosting round steak

Trim excess fat from meat. Cut 1½ pounds boneless beef round steak into 4 portions. To wrap for freezing, place 2 layers of waxed

STEAKS & CHOPS

SPINACH-STUFFED ROUND STEAK

Total cooking time: 50 minutes

- 1 10-ounce package frozen chopped spinach, thawed and well drained
- 2 tablespoons sliced green onion
- 1 tablespoon butter or margarine
- 1 slightly beaten egg
- ⅓ cup grated Parmesan cheese
- ¾ teaspoon dried marjoram, crushed
- 1½ pounds beef top round steak, cut ½ to ¾ inch thick
- 1 7½-ounce can semicondensed savory cream of mushroom soup
- 2 tablespoons sliced green onion
- 1 tablespoon milk
- 1 tablespoon dry sherry

For stuffing, in 1-quart casserole combine spinach, 2 tablespoons green onion, and butter. Cook, uncovered, at **HIGH** for 3 minutes till vegetables are crisp-tender. Stir in egg, Parmesan cheese, and marjoram. Set aside. Trim excess fat from meat. Pound to ¼-inch thickness. Spread stuffing over meat. Roll up jelly-roll style, beginning with the short side. Tie with string. Place seam side up on a nonmetal rack in 12x7½x2-inch baking dish. Cook meat roll, uncovered, at **HIGH** for 5 minutes. Cook at **MEDIUM or COOK POWER 5 (50%)** for 15 minutes. Turn stuffed steak roll over; give dish a half turn. Cook at **MEDIUM or COOK POWER 5 (50%)** for 15 minutes till meat is tender and reaches internal temperature of 140°F when tested with meat thermometer, giving dish a half turn once. Cover with foil and let stand, shiny side in, for 10 minutes. Meanwhile, for sauce, in 2-cup glass measure stir together soup, remaining green onion, milk, and sherry. Cook at **HIGH** for 2 minutes till hot, stirring once. Remove string from steak roll; carve. Pass sauce. Serves 6.

LAMB CHOPS OLÉ

Total cooking time: 22 minutes

- ½ medium onion, sliced
- ¼ cup chopped green pepper
- ¼ cup sliced celery
- 2 tablespoons water
- 1 8-ounce can tomato sauce
- ½ small clove garlic, minced
- ½ teaspoon chili powder
  Dash bottled hot pepper sauce
- 2 shoulder lamb chops
  Hot cooked noodles

In a 10x6x2-inch baking dish combine the onion, green pepper, and celery. Add water. Cook at **HIGH** for 2 minutes. Add tomato sauce, garlic, chili powder, and hot pepper sauce. Dip lamb chops in mixture to coat, then arrange atop mixture. Cover; cook at **MEDIUM or COOK POWER 5 (50%)** for 20 minutes, turning chops over after 10 minutes. Serve sauce over hot cooked noodles. Makes 2 servings.

HAM CARIBBEAN

Total cooking time: 22 minutes, 30 seconds

- ¼ cup packed brown sugar
- 1 tablespoon cornstarch
- ⅛ teaspoon ground cloves
- ½ cup orange juice
- 2 tablespoons honey
- 2 tablespoons rum
- 1 2-pound fully cooked ham slice
- 4 bananas, halved crosswise and lengthwise

In 2-cup glass measure combine brown sugar, cornstarch, and cloves; mix well. Stir in orange juice, honey, and rum. Cook, uncovered, at **HIGH** for 2½ minutes till thickened and bubbly, stirring after each minute. Set aside. Place ham slice in 12x7½x2-inch baking dish. Cover with waxed paper. Cook at **MEDIUM HIGH or COOK POWER 7 (70%)** for 9 minutes. Turn ham slice over; drain if necessary. Pour sauce over ham. Cook, covered, at **MEDIUM HIGH or COOK POWER 7 (70%)** for 7 minutes. Add bananas to dish, turning to coat with sauce. Continue cooking, covered, at **MEDIUM HIGH or COOK POWER 7 (70%)** for 4 minutes till hot. Spoon sauce over. Makes 8 servings.

Defrosting roasts

Place an unwrapped frozen 4-pound boneless beef rolled rib roast in a baking dish; cover loosely with waxed paper. (Or, if the roast was prepackaged in freezer paper, begin defrosting in the wrapper.) Defrost according to directions on page 32. Halfway through defrosting time, turn roast over; continue defrosting for remainder of the time.

Test for thawing doneness by piercing the roast in the center and at the sides with a long-tined fork. If you can push the fork into the center of the roast using moderate pressure, it is ready for the suggested standing time. If the roast feels solid in the middle, a few more minutes of defrosting time are needed.

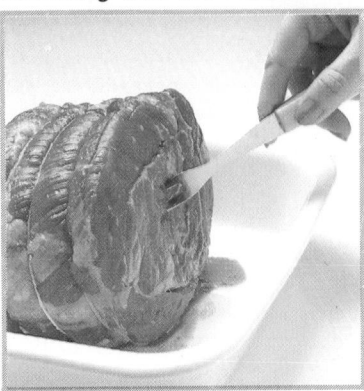

Microwave oven roasting

Place beef rib roast, fat side down, in microwave roasting pan with rack or in a 12x7½x2-inch baking dish with a roasting rack. Cover roast with waxed paper. Cook at Medium High or Cook Power 7 (70%) for 30 minutes.

Turn roast over; give dish a half turn. Insert a microwave meat thermometer or a temperature probe into center of largest muscle. Continue cooking at Medium High or Cook Power 7 (70%) to desired doneness (refer to exact timings in chart opposite). Shield areas that are browning too quickly with small pieces of foil. Remove roast from microwave oven. Cover, or tent, with foil; let stand 10 minutes. The internal temperature should rise 10°F.

ROASTING CHART

To ensure even cooking of roasts, select cuts that are evenly shaped and trim excess fat. During the cooking time, some parts of the roast may cook and brown more quickly than others. Shield these portions with small pieces of foil as necessary.
*Do not use a conventional thermometer inside the microwave oven. Special microwave thermometers are available.

MEAT	WEIGHT	TOTAL COOKING TIME	REGULAR METHOD	TEMPERATURE PROBE METHOD
Standing Beef Rib Roast	5 pounds	50 to 60 minutes for rare, 60 to 65 minutes for medium doneness at **MEDIUM HIGH or COOK POWER 7 (70%)**	1. Choose an evenly shaped 3-rib roast, cut from the small end. (It should measure about 6 inches wide, 6½ inches long, and 3¾ inches tall.) If necessary, trim excess fat. Season the roast with some salt and pepper. Place roast, bone side up, on microwave roasting rack in 12x7½x2-inch baking dish. Cover roast loosely with waxed paper.	
			2. Cook at **MEDIUM HIGH or COOK POWER 7 (70%)** for 30 minutes. Turn roast, fat side up, and give dish a half turn. Cover any overbrown areas with foil, securing with wooden toothpicks.	
			3. Re-cover roast with waxed paper; cook at **MEDIUM HIGH or COOK POWER 7 (70%)** for remaining cooking time or till a meat thermometer* registers 130°F for rare, 140° to 145°F for medium doneness.	3. Insert the temperature probe into the center of largest muscle, not touching fat or bone. Re-cover with waxed paper and cook at **MEDIUM HIGH or COOK POWER 7 (70%)** to 130°F for rare, 140° to 145°F for medium doneness.
			4. Remove waxed paper. Cover the roast with foil and let it stand on the counter for 10 minutes. The temperature should register 140°F for rare, 150°F for medium doneness. The outside of the roast will be well done. If you desire more well-done meat, slice the roast, then cook the rare or medium slices at **MEDIUM HIGH or COOK POWER 7 (70%)** for a few more minutes.	
Boneless Beef Rolled Rib Roast	4 pounds	44 to 50 minutes for rare, 50 to 55 minutes for medium doneness at **MEDIUM HIGH or COOK POWER 7 (70%)**	1. Choose an evenly shaped roast, cut from the small end. (It should measure about 4 inches wide, 6½ inches long, and 4 inches tall.) If necessary, untie roast and trim excess fat from outside of roast; retie with heavy string. Season with salt and pepper. Place, fat side down, on microwave roasting rack in 12x7½x2-inch baking dish. Cover loosely with waxed paper.	
			2. Cook at **MEDIUM HIGH or COOK POWER 7 (70%)** for 30 minutes. Turn roast, fat side up, and give dish a half turn. Cover any overbrown areas with foil, securing with wooden toothpicks.	
			3. Re-cover roast with waxed paper; cook at **MEDIUM HIGH or COOK POWER 7 (70%)** for remaining cooking time till meat thermometer* registers 130°F for rare, 140° to 145°F for medium doneness.	3. Insert temperature probe into center of largest muscle. Re-cover the roast with waxed paper and cook at **MEDIUM HIGH or COOK POWER 7 (70%)** to 130°F for rare, 140° to 145°F for medium doneness.
			4. Remove the waxed paper. Cover the roast with foil and let it stand on the counter for 10 minutes. The temperature should register 140°F for rare, 150°F for medium doneness. The outside of the roast will be well done. If you desire more well-done meat, slice the roast, then cook the rare or medium slices at **MEDIUM HIGH or COOK POWER (70%)** for a few more minutes.	

ROASTING CHART

MEAT	WEIGHT	TOTAL COOKING TIME	REGULAR METHOD	TEMPERATURE PROBE METHOD
Fully Cooked Boneless Ham	3 pounds	40 to 45 minutes at **MEDIUM or COOK POWER 5 (50%)**	1. Tie the ham with heavy string, if necessary. Cap the edges of ham on top and bottom with small strips of foil; secure the foil with wooden toothpicks. Place the ham, fat side down, on a microwave roasting rack in a 12x7½x2-inch baking dish. Cover the ham loosely with waxed paper.	
	4 pounds	55 to 60 minutes at **MEDIUM or COOK POWER 5 (50%)**	2. Cook the ham at **MEDIUM or COOK POWER 5 (50%)** for *half* of the cooking time. Turn the ham over and give the baking dish a half turn.	
	5 pounds	60 to 70 minutes at **MEDIUM or COOK POWER 5 (50%)**	3. Re-cover the ham with waxed paper and continue cooking at **MEDIUM or COOK POWER 5 (50%)** for the remaining half of the cooking time or till a meat thermometer* registers 120° to 125°F. If desired, glaze ham during the last 5 minutes of cooking.	3. Insert the temperature probe into the center of the largest muscle. Re-cover the ham with waxed paper and cook at **MEDIUM or COOK POWER 5 (50%)** to 120° to 125°F. If desired, glaze the ham during the last 5 minutes of cooking.
			4. Remove the waxed paper and foil strips from the ham. Cover the ham with foil and let it stand on the counter top for 5 to 10 minutes. The temperature, measured with a meat thermometer*, should register 130°F.	
Canned Ham	3 pounds	40 to 45 minutes at **MEDIUM or COOK POWER 5 (50%)**	1. Tie the ham with heavy string. Cap edges of ham on top and bottom with small strips of foil; secure with wooden toothpicks. Place ham, fat side down, on microwave roasting rack in 12x7½x2-inch baking dish. Cover ham loosely with waxed paper.	
	5 pounds	1 hour 10 minutes to 1 hour 15 minutes at **MEDIUM or COOK POWER 5 (50%)**	2. Cook the ham at **MEDIUM or COOK POWER 5 (50%)** for *half* of the cooking time. Turn the ham over and give the baking dish a half turn.	
			3. Re-cover the ham with waxed paper; continue cooking ham at **MEDIUM or COOK POWER 5 (50%)** for the remaining half of the cooking time or until a meat thermometer* registers 120° to 125°F. If desired, glaze the ham during the last 5 minutes of cooking.	3. Insert the temperature probe into center of the largest muscle. Re-cover the ham with waxed paper and cook at **MEDIUM or COOK POWER 5 (50%)** to 120° to 125°F. If desired, glaze the ham during the last 5 minutes of cooking.
			4. Remove the waxed paper and foil strips from the ham. Cover the ham with foil and let it stand on the counter top for 5 to 10 minutes. The temperature, measured with a meat thermometer*, should register 130°F.	

*Do not use a conventional thermometer inside the microwave oven. Special microwave thermometers are available. Do not use a microwave meat thermometer in a conventional oven.

ROASTS

MARINATED ROAST LEG OF LAMB

Total cooking time: 60 to 71 minutes

- 1 5- to 6-pound leg of lamb
- ⅓ cup dry red wine
- ¼ cup cooking oil
- ¼ cup Worcestershire sauce
- 3 cloves garlic, minced

Remove excess fat from lamb. Place lamb in a large, heavy plastic cooking bag. Place bag in a shallow baking dish. Combine wine, oil, Worcestershire sauce, and garlic. Pour over lamb in bag. Close bag; chill in the refrigerator for several hours or overnight to marinate, turning bag occasionally. Remove lamb from bag, reserving marinade. Place lamb on a microwave baking rack in a 12x7½x2-inch baking dish. Place in microwave oven. Cook at **HIGH** for 5 minutes. Cover; cook at **MEDIUM or COOK POWER 5 (50%)** for 11 minutes per pound of lamb till internal temperature reaches 140°F for medium doneness, giving dish a half turn every 15 minutes and turning meat over and brushing with marinade after 25 minutes. Cover with foil; let stand 10 minutes before carving. The temperature, measured with a meat thermometer, should register 150°F. Makes 6 to 8 servings.

ITALIAN-STYLE POT ROAST

Total cooking time: 1 hour, 43 minutes

- 1 3-pound beef chuck pot roast
- ½ cup water
- 1 tablespoon Worcestershire sauce
- 1 teaspoon instant beef bouillon granules
- 1 clove garlic, minced
- ½ teaspoon salt
- ½ teaspoon sugar
- ½ teaspoon dried oregano, crushed
- ¼ teaspoon pepper
- 3 medium carrots, cut into strips
- 3 medium potatoes, peeled and cut into 1-inch cubes
- 3 stalks celery, cut into 2-inch pieces
- 2 medium onions, quartered
- 1 8-ounce can tomato sauce
- ¼ cup all-purpose flour
- 1 4-ounce can mushroom stems and pieces, drained

Trim excess fat from meat. In a 3-quart casserole stir together next 8 ingredients; add the meat. Place in microwave oven. Cover roast and cook at **HIGH** for 5 minutes. Cook at **MEDIUM or COOK POWER 5 (50%)** for 50 minutes. Turn roast over; add carrots, potatoes, celery, and onions. Cover and cook meat and vegetables at **MEDIUM or COOK POWER 5** for 40 minutes or till meat and vegetables are tender, spooning broth mixture over vegetables twice during cooking. Remove meat and vegetables to serving platter. Skim fat from broth mixture. Stir together tomato sauce and flour; stir into broth mixture along with mushrooms. Cook, uncovered, at **HIGH** for 7 minutes till bubbly, stirring every minute. Cook, uncovered, at **HIGH** for 1 minute. Spoon some of the tomato mixture over meat and vegetables on platter; pass remaining tomato mixture. Makes 8 servings.

ROASTS

Microwave thermometers

For safety's sake, do not use a conventional meat thermometer inside a microwave oven. Invest in a microwave oven thermometer.

Remember you should use a microwave oven thermometer only in a microwave oven, never in a conventional oven. You may check the roast temperature outside the microwave oven with a microwave oven or conventional oven thermometer, allowing 1 minute for the temperature to register.

Remember to remove the conventional oven meat thermometer from the food before continuing to cook in the microwave oven.

FREEZER-TO-TABLE POT ROAST

Total cooking time: About 1 hour, 45 minutes

- 1 3- to 3½-pound frozen beef chuck pot roast, unwrapped
- ½ cup dairy sour cream
- 2 tablespoons all-purpose flour
- 1 4-ounce can mushroom stems and pieces, drained
- 1 1¼-ounce envelope regular onion soup mix

To loosen wrapping, run under water; pat dry. Place roast in 12x7½x2-inch baking dish. Cover with vented plastic wrap; cook at **HIGH** for 3 minutes. Cook at **MEDIUM or COOK POWER 5 (50%)** for 15 minutes *per pound*, giving dish a half turn after 25 minutes; drain. Cover; cook at **MEDIUM or COOK POWER 5 (50%)** for 4½ minutes *per pound*. Combine sour cream and flour. Add mushrooms and soup mix. Stir in 1½ cups *water*. Pour over roast. Cover; cook at **MEDIUM or COOK POWER 5 (50%)** for 14 minutes *per pound*. Remove meat. Skim excess fat from sauce, if necessary. Makes 8 servings.

ORIENTAL MARINATED BEEF

Total cooking time: 1 hour, 31 minutes

- 1 3-pound beef chuck pot roast
- 4 green onions, sliced
- ¼ cup soy sauce
- ¼ cup vinegar
- 2 tablespoons honey
- 1 teaspoon ground ginger
- 1 clove garlic, minced
- 1 tablespoon cornstarch

Trim fat from meat. Use tines of fork to pierce meat on both sides. Place meat and onions in plastic bag; set in 12x7½x2-inch baking dish. Combine next 5 ingredients and 2 tablespoons *water;* pour over meat and onions in bag and close. Marinate in refrigerator for several hours or overnight, turning occasionally. Remove meat, onions, and marinade from bag; return to dish. Place in microwave oven. Cover with vented plastic wrap; cook at **HIGH** for 5 minutes. Cook at **MEDIUM or COOK POWER 5 (50%)** for 30 minutes. Turn roast over. Cover; cook at **MEDIUM or**

COOK POWER 5 (50%) for 40 minutes till tender, giving dish a half turn once. Remove meat from dish. Cover with foil; let stand 10 minutes. Meanwhile, skim fat from juices in dish. Measure 1 cup juices; return the 1 cup juices to dish. Stir together cornstarch and ¼ cup *cold water.* Stir cornstarch mixture into juices. Cook, uncovered, at **HIGH** for 6 minutes till bubbly, stirring every minute. Pass marinade with meat. Makes 8 servings.

BURGUNDY-BERRIED HAM

Total cooking time: 12 minutes

- ½ cup cranberry orange sauce
- 2 tablespoons packed brown sugar
- 2 tablespoons burgundy or dry red wine
- 1 teaspoon prepared mustard
- 1 1½-pound canned ham, cut into ¼-inch-thick slices

In a 2-cup glass measure combine all ingredients except ham. Cook berry mixture, uncovered, at **HIGH** for 2 minutes till heated through, stirring after 1 minute. Place ham in 12x7½x2-inch baking dish overlapping slices to fit; pour berry mixture over. Cover; cook at **MEDIUM HIGH or COOK POWER 7 (70%)** for 10 minutes, giving dish half turn once. Serves 6.

CORNED BEEF WITH PEACH GLAZE

Total cooking time: 2 hours, 15 minutes

- 1 3-pound corned beef brisket
- 1 bay leaf
- 1 29-ounce can peach halves
- ¼ cup packed brown sugar
- ¼ cup catsup
- 2 tablespoons vinegar
- 2 teaspoons prepared mustard

Place brisket in 4-quart casserole. Add water to cover (about 7 cups), bay leaf, and seasonings from brisket package. Cover; cook at **MEDIUM or COOK POWER 5 (50%)** for 2 hours till tender, turning once. Cool 10 minutes; slice across grain and place in 12x7½x2-inch baking dish. Drain fruit, reserving ¼ cup syrup; arrange fruit around meat. Blend syrup and remaining ingredients; pour over all. Cover; cook at **MEDIUM or COOK POWER 5 (50%)** for 15 minutes. Makes 8 to 10 servings.

58

Poultry

Poultry is one of today's best food bargains. It's nutritious, economical, and low in calories and cholesterol. And, poultry cooked in your Whirlpool microwave oven will come out tender, flavorful and juicy in just minutes. This chapter is full of recipes to help you make the most of fresh and frozen chicken, duckling, and turkey.

Cooking

When a recipe calls for cooked chicken, turn to your microwave oven to cook it fast. In twelve minutes or less, a pound of chicken is ready, tender, and juicy. Also use this method for small servings of chicken for children or dieters. Flavor with a sprinkle of herbs, a sprig of parsley, or a slice or two of carrot, celery, or onion; add salt and pepper before serving.

Start with 1 pound of meaty chicken breasts, skin and bones still intact. Place in a 1½- or 2-quart casserole and add 1 tablespoon water. Cook, covered, at High for 6 to 7 minutes, turning chicken over after 4 minutes. Cool and cube. Makes 1 cup cubed cooked chicken.

Cook 1½ pounds of meaty chicken breasts for 9 to 10 minutes. It should yield 1½ cups cubed cooked chicken.

Cook 2 pounds of meaty chicken breasts for 10 to 12 minutes. It should yield 2 cups cubed cooked chicken.

Coatings

Poultry does not brown well or crisp in the short time it requires to cook. There are a variety of ways to add color and appeal. Chicken pieces may be coated with herbs or one of many crumb coatings, or brushed with a barbecue sauce or butter-paprika mixture before cooking.

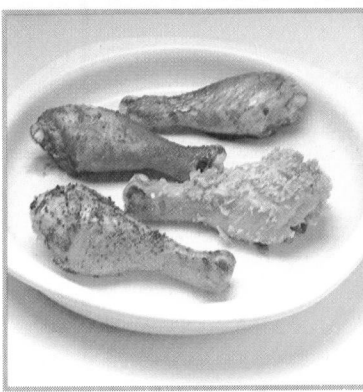

Because of its irregular shape, poultry may brown unevenly. Brushing with equal parts of Kitchen Bouquet and melted butter or margarine will give the chicken a deeper color and more attractive appearance than if cooked plain.

Defrosting pieces

Chicken pieces thaw faster when separated. Defrost according to defrosting directions given on pages 32-34. Test for thawing doneness by piercing the center of meaty portions of chicken. Remove thawed portions; add a few more minutes to defrost pieces that are still firm. Chicken pieces should be completely thawed *before* cooking.

Arranging to cook

Arrange chicken pieces from a 2½- to 3-pound broiler-fryer in a baking dish, with thickest, meatiest portions to the outside and corners of the dish. Rearrange the pieces once so that less-cooked portions are moved to outside of the dish.

Cover to cook

Cover the baking dish with a sheet of waxed paper to hold in some steam for more even cooking and to prevent spattering of fat and juices in oven cavity.

Doneness test

To test chicken pieces for cooking doneness, pierce a meaty portion with a fork or make a small slit with a sharp knife.

The meat should be tender and moist with no pink tinge; the meat juices should be clear. Remember to remove the less-meaty portions from baking dish to prevent overcooking.

PIECES

CHICKEN AND RICE CASSEROLE

Total cooking time: 25 minutes

- ¾ cup water
- 1 cup uncooked quick-cooking rice
- ½ cup chopped celery
- ¼ cup chopped onion
- 2 tablespoons water
- 1 10¾-ounce can condensed cream of chicken soup or cream of mushroom soup
- ½ teaspoon dried thyme, crushed
- 8 chicken thighs, skinned
  Paprika

In a 2-cup glass measure heat the ¾ cup water at **HIGH** for 1 to 2 minutes till boiling. Stir in rice; cover with plastic wrap and set aside. In a medium bowl combine celery, onion, and the 2 tablespoons water. Cook, covered with waxed paper, at **HIGH** for 5 minutes till tender; drain. Stir in soup, thyme, and ⅛ teaspoon *pepper.* Spread rice in a 8x8x2-inch baking dish. Arrange the chicken pieces, boney side up, on rice layer. Spread the soup mixture over all. Cook, covered with waxed paper, at **HIGH** for 10 minutes. Turn chicken over and re-arrange so the least-cooked portions are to outside of dish. Cook, covered, at **HIGH** for 9 minutes till chicken is tender. Sprinkle with paprika. Makes 4 servings.

CRANBERRY BARBECUED CHICKEN

Total cooking time: 25 minutes

- 1 8-ounce can whole cranberry sauce
- ½ cup finely chopped onion
- ½ cup catsup
- ¼ cup finely chopped celery
- 4 teaspoons cornstarch
- 2 tablespoons lemon juice
- 1 tablespoon brown sugar
- 1 tablespoon prepared mustard
- 1 tablespoon Worcestershire sauce
- 1 tablespoon vinegar
- 1 2½- to 3-pound broiler-fryer chicken, cut up

In a 12x7½x2-inch baking dish combine whole cranberry sauce, onion, catsup, celery, cornstarch, lemon juice, brown sugar, mustard, Worcestershire sauce, and vinegar. Add chicken pieces, skin side down, to sauce in dish. Turn chicken pieces, skin side up, to coat with sauce, placing meaty pieces toward outside of dish. Sprinkle with salt. Cover with waxed paper; cook at **MEDIUM HIGH or COOK POWER 7 (70%)** for 25 minutes till tender, turning dish once. Remove chicken to a serving platter. Skim fat from sauce. Stir sauce and spoon some over chicken; pass remaining sauce. Makes 6 servings.

GINGER-ORANGE CHICKEN

Total cooking time: 23 minutes, 30 seconds

- 1 2½- to 3-pound broiler-fryer chicken, cut up
- 1 teaspoon salt
- ¼ teaspoon paprika
- ½ of 6-ounce can (⅓ cup) frozen orange juice concentrate, thawed
- ⅓ cup water
- 2 tablespoons brown sugar
- 2 tablespoons snipped parsley
- 2 teaspoons soy sauce
- ½ teaspoon ground ginger
- 1 tablespoon cornstarch
- 1 tablespoon cold water
  Hot cooked rice
  Orange slices
  Paprika

Arrange chicken in 12x7½x2-inch baking dish so meatiest portions are toward outside of dish. Sprinkle with salt and paprika. In 2-cup measure combine orange concentrate, water, brown sugar, parsley, soy, and ginger; pour over chicken. Cover and cook at **MEDIUM HIGH or COOK POWER 7 (70%)** for 20 minutes till tender. Remove chicken to platter. Cover; keep warm. Skim fat from pan juices. In small bowl combine cornstarch and water. Add to pan juices in baking dish. Cook at **HIGH** for 3½ minutes till thickened and bubbly, stirring after each minute. Spoon sauce over chicken. Serve with rice. Garnish with twisted orange slices and parsley. Makes 6 servings.

CHICKEN ENCHILADAS

Total cooking time: 6 minutes, 30 seconds

- 6 corn tortillas, thawed
- 1/4 cup cooking oil
- 2 tablespoons butter or margarine
- 2 tablespoons all-purpose flour
- Dash paprika
- Dash ground nutmeg
- Dash salt
- Dash pepper
- 1/2 cup chicken broth
- 3/4 cup shredded Monterey Jack or cheddar cheese
- 2 teaspoons lemon juice
- 1 tablespoon snipped parsley
- 1/2 teaspoon grated onion
- 1 cup finely diced cooked chicken
- Avocado Sauce (recipe below)
- Jalapeño Relish (recipe below)

Cook tortillas in hot oil in skillet on top of range for 10 seconds on each side, just till limp. Set aside on paper toweling. In 4-cup glass measure heat butter or margarine at **HIGH** for 30 seconds till melted. Blend in flour and seasonings. Add chicken broth. Cook, uncovered, at **HIGH** for 2 minutes till thickened and bubbly, stirring every 30 seconds. Add 1/4 cup of the cheese, the lemon juice, parsley, and onion; stir in chicken. Divide chicken mixture among tortillas; roll up and place in 12x7 1/2x2-inch baking dish. Cover and cook at **MEDIUM HIGH or COOK POWER 7 (70%)** for 3 minutes. Sprinkle enchiladas with remaining 1/2 cup cheese. Cook, uncovered, at **HIGH** for 1 minute till cheese melts. Pass Avocado Sauce and Jalapeño Relish. Makes 3 servings.

Avocado Sauce: Seed and peel 1 *avocado;* place in a small bowl and mash. Stir in 1/4 cup dairy *sour cream,* 2 teaspoons *lemon juice,* 1/8 teaspoon *salt,* dash *onion powder,* and 5 drops *bottled hot pepper sauce.*

Jalapeño Relish: In a small bowl blend 1 small *tomato,* finely chopped; 2 tablespoons finely chopped *onion;* 1 *jalapeño or green chili pepper,* finely chopped; and 1/4 teaspoon *salt.* Chill before serving.

TURKEY DIVAN

Total cooking time: 21 minutes, 30 seconds

- 2 10-ounce packages frozen chopped broccoli
- 2 tablespoons butter or margarine
- 3 tablespoons all-purpose flour
- 1/2 teaspoon salt
- 2 cups milk
- 1/4 cup shredded Swiss cheese
- 2 cups cooked turkey or chicken cut into strips
- 1/4 cup grated Parmesan cheese

Place broccoli in 10x6x2-inch baking dish. Cover and cook at **HIGH** for 10 minutes, breaking up and stirring twice. Drain well. Cover and set aside. In 4-cup glass measure heat butter at **HIGH** for 30 seconds till melted. Stir in flour and salt. Add milk all at once. Cook at **HIGH** for 6 minutes till thickened and bubbly, stirring after each minute. Stir in Swiss cheese till melted. Place turkey atop broccoli in baking dish. Pour cheese sauce over turkey. Sprinkle with Parmesan cheese. Cover and cook at **MEDIUM HIGH or COOK POWER 7 (70%)** for 5 minutes till heated through. Makes 6 servings.

CHICKEN AND CHIPS CASSEROLE

Total cooking time: 9 minutes

- 2 cups cubed cooked chicken or turkey
- 2 cups sliced celery
- 1/3 cup toasted slivered almonds
- 2 teaspoons grated onion
- 1/2 teaspoon salt
- 3/4 cup mayonnaise or salad dressing
- 2 tablespoons lemon juice
- 1/2 cup shredded American cheese
- 1 cup crushed potato chips

In medium bowl combine chicken, celery, almonds, onion, and salt. In small bowl combine mayonnaise and lemon juice. Stir mayonnaise mixture into chicken mixture. Spread chicken mixture evenly in 8x1 1/2-inch round baking dish. Cover and cook at **HIGH** for 8 minutes, stirring after 4 minutes. Stir again and sprinkle with cheese. Cook at **HIGH** for 1 minute. Sprinkle with potato chips. Makes 6 servings.

COOKED

CREAMED CHICKEN

Total cooking time: 7 minutes, 45 seconds

- ¼ cup butter or margarine
- ⅓ cup all-purpose flour
- ½ teaspoon salt
- 1 cup chicken broth
- 1 cup milk
- 2 cups cubed cooked chicken
- 1 3-ounce can sliced mushrooms, drained
- ¼ cup chopped pimiento
  Toasted English muffins

In a 1½-quart casserole heat butter at **HIGH** for 45 seconds till melted. Stir in flour and salt. Add broth and milk. Cook on **HIGH** for 5 minutes till thickened and bubbly, stirring after each minute. Blend in chicken, mushrooms, and pimiento. Cook at **HIGH** for 2 minutes till hot. Serve over toasted English muffins. Makes 4 servings.

FRIED RICE BUNDLES

Total cooking time: 8 minutes, 30 seconds

- ¼ cup sliced green onion
- 2 tablespoons cooking oil
- 2 cups cooked rice
- 1 4½-ounce can tiny shrimp, drained
- 1 cup cubed cooked chicken
- 1 cup fresh or canned bean sprouts
- ½ cup sliced water chestnuts
- 3 tablespoons soy sauce
- ⅛ teaspoon pepper
- 1 tablespoon cooking oil
- 2 slightly beaten eggs
- 12 lettuce leaves

In a large glass bowl combine onion and 2 tablespoons oil. Cook at **HIGH** for 2 minutes. Add cooked rice, shrimp, chicken, bean sprouts, water chestnuts, soy sauce, and pepper. Cook at **HIGH** for 5 minutes, stirring twice. Cover with foil to keep warm. Place remaining 1 tablespoon oil in pie plate. Add eggs. Cook at **HIGH** for 1½ minutes, stirring every 30 seconds. Cut up large pieces of egg. Stir egg into rice mixture. To serve, spoon portions of hot rice mixture into lettuce leaves, roll up. Serve with Chinese plum sauce or hoisin sauce, if desired. Makes 6 servings.

MEXICAN CHEF'S SALAD

Total cooking time: 3 minutes

- 6 cups torn lettuce
- 1 cup shredded carrot (2 carrots)
- 1 cup finely chopped celery (2 stalks)
- 1 cup cooked ham cut in julienne strips
- 1 cup cooked chicken cut in julienne strips
- 2 medium tomatoes, chopped
- ¼ cup sliced pitted ripe olives
- 3 tablespoons sliced green onion
- 2 cups shredded American cheese (8 ounces)
- ½ cup milk
- ¼ cup chopped canned green chili peppers
- 2 cups corn chips

In large salad bowl combine lettuce, carrot, and celery. Arrange ham, chicken, tomatoes, olives, and green onion atop. In 4-cup glass measure combine cheese and milk. Cook at **MEDIUM or COOK POWER 5 (50%)** for 3 minutes, stirring twice. Stir till smooth. Stir in chili peppers; pour over salad. Toss lightly. Serve at once. Pass corn chips to sprinkle atop. Makes 6 servings.

Note: If desired, cheese sauce may be made ahead and served cold. Increase milk in sauce to ¾ cup. Chill till serving time. If sauce is too thick, stir in a little milk.

CHICKEN TAMALE PIE

Total cooking time: 17 minutes

- 1 11-ounce can condensed cheddar cheese soup
- 1 8-ounce can tomato sauce
- 2 5-ounce cans chicken, flaked, or 1½ cups cubed cooked chicken
- ¾ cup uncooked minute-type rice
- 2 15-ounce cans tamales

In an 8x8x2-inch baking dish combine cheese soup, tomato sauce, chicken, and rice. Cover; cook at **HIGH** for 2½ minutes. Stir and cook at **HIGH** for 2½ minutes. Drain tamales, reserving liquid. Stir reserved liquid into soup mixture. Arrange tamales atop. Cover; cook at **HIGH** for 12 minutes till rice is done. Makes 6 servings.

Tips & Techniques

Defrosting test

Refer to defrosting directions for poultry on pages 32-34. Test for thawing doneness by piercing the center of a leg or breast with a long-tined meat fork. If the meat is difficult to pierce, a few more minutes of microwave defrosting time are needed. Poultry should be completely thawed *before* cooking.

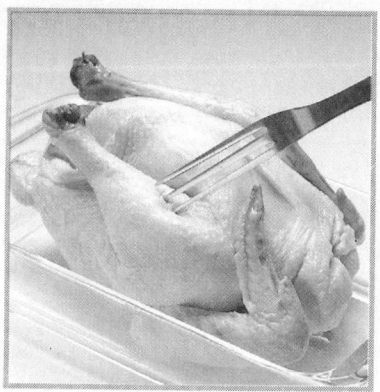

Shielding

About halfway through the cooking time, when the chicken is turned breast side up, shield bony parts to prevent overcooking. Cover wing tips and legs with small pieces of foil. Secure with wooden picks, if necessary.

Covering

Cover chicken with a loose tent of waxed paper during cooking. This covering helps retain heat for more even cooking and prevents spatters in the oven.

Standing time

Cover cooked poultry with a sheet of foil to retain heat during standing time. Let stand on counter top 10 to 15 minutes before serving. A meat thermometer inserted in the inside thigh muscle should register 175°F after removal from the oven and 185°F after the standing time.

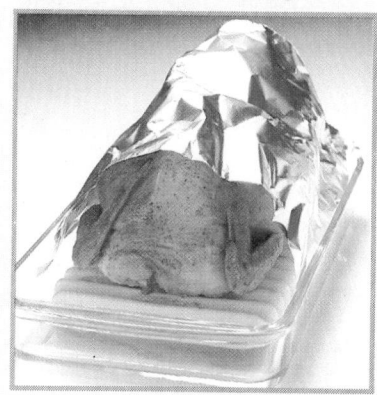

POULTRY ROASTING CHART

TYPE BIRD	WEIGHT	TOTAL COOKING TIME	METHOD
Whole Broiler-Fryer Chicken	3 pounds	9 minutes at **HIGH,** then 30 to 32 minutes at **MEDIUM or COOK POWER 5 (50%)**	*Make sure chicken is completely defrosted.* Tie legs together and wings close to body with heavy string. Place chicken, breast side down, on microwave roasting rack in 12x7½x2-inch baking dish. Cover with loose tent of waxed paper. Cook chicken at **HIGH** for 9 minutes. Continue cooking chicken, breast side down, at **MEDIUM or COOK POWER 5 (50%)** for 16 minutes. Turn chicken, breast side up, and give baking dish a half turn. Cover legs and wings with foil; secure with wooden toothpicks. Re-cover chicken with loose tent of waxed paper and cook at **MEDIUM or COOK POWER 5 (50%)** for remaining cooking time or till meat thermometer* inserted in the inside thigh muscle, not touching bone, registers 175°F. Cover with foil. Let stand 10 to 15 minutes. Thermometer* should register 180° to 185°F. If any portion of chicken is not quite done, slice and return just that portion to microwave oven and cook at **MEDIUM HIGH or COOK POWER 7 (70%)** a few minutes.
Whole Turkey	8 pounds	40 minutes at **HIGH,** then 40 minutes at **MEDIUM or COOK POWER 5 (50%)**	*Make sure the turkey is completely defrosted.* (If ice crystals remain, rinse cavity with cold water and drain thoroughly.) Tie the legs together and wings close to body with heavy string. Place the turkey, breast side down, on a microwave roasting rack in 12x7½x2-inch baking dish. Cover the legs and wings with foil; secure foil with wooden toothpicks. Cover the turkey with a loose tent of waxed paper. Cook turkey at **HIGH** for 20 minutes. Turn the turkey, breast side up, and cook at **HIGH** for 20 minutes. Turn the turkey, breast side down, and give the baking dish a half turn. Remove the foil from legs and wings. Then cook at **MEDIUM or COOK POWER 5 (50%)** for the remainder of the cooking time or till meat thermometer* inserted in the center of the inside thigh muscle, not touching bone, registers 175°F. Cover the turkey with foil and let stand for 10 to 15 minutes. Thermometer* should register 180° to 185°F. If any portion of turkey is not quite done, slice and return just that portion to the microwave oven and cook at **MEDIUM HIGH or COOK POWER 7 (70%)** for a few minutes.
Turkey Breast	5 pounds	1¼ to 1½ hours at **MEDIUM HIGH or COOK POWER 7 (70%)**	*Make sure turkey breast is completely defrosted.* Trim away excess fat. Place turkey breast, skin side down, on microwave roasting rack in 12x7½x2-inch baking dish. Cover breast with loose tent of waxed paper. Cook turkey breast at **MEDIUM HIGH or COOK POWER 7 (70%)** for 50 minutes. Turn turkey breast skin down again. Cook, covered, at **MEDIUM HIGH or COOK POWER 7 (70%)** for remaining cooking time or till meat thermometer* inserted in meatiest portion of breast registers 175°F. Cover with foil. Let stand 10 to 15 minutes. Thermometer* should register 180° to 185°F.

*Do not use a conventional thermometer inside the microwave oven. Special microwave thermometers are available. Do not use a microwave meat thermometer in a conventional oven.

TYPE BIRD	WEIGHT	TOTAL COOKING TIME	METHOD
Boneless Turkey Roast	3 pounds	45 to 50 minutes at **MEDIUM HIGH or COOK POWER 7 (70%)**	If turkey roast is frozen, *defrost completely* according to defrosting instructions on page 33. Place turkey roast, skin side down, on a microwave roasting rack in a 12x7½x2-inch baking dish. Cover with a loose tent of waxed paper. Cook at **MEDIUM HIGH or COOK POWER 7 (70%)** for 20 minutes. Turn roast over. Cook at **MEDIUM HIGH or COOK POWER 7 (70%)** for the remainder of the cooking time or till a meat thermometer* inserted in the center of turkey roast registers 170°F. Let stand for 15 minutes before serving. Thermometer* should register 180 to 185°F.
Duckling	5 pounds	44 minutes at **MEDIUM HIGH or COOK POWER 7 (70%)**	*Make sure duckling is completely defrosted.* Prick skin all over. Tie legs together and wings close to body with heavy string. Place the duckling, breast side down, on a microwave roasting rack in a 12x7½x2-inch baking dish. Cover loosely with waxed paper. Cook duckling at **MEDIUM HIGH or COOK POWER 7 (70%)** for 20 minutes. Drain off the excess fat and turn the duckling breast side up. Cook, loosely covered, at **MEDIUM HIGH or COOK POWER 7 (70%)** for the remainder of the cooking time or till a meat thermometer* inserted in the center of the inside thigh muscle, not touching bone, registers 175°F. Cover duckling with foil and let it stand on the counter for 10 to 15 minutes. Thermometer* should register 180° to 185°F.
Cornish Hens	1 (1¼ pounds)	12 minutes at **MEDIUM HIGH or COOK POWER 7 (70%)**	*Make sure hen is completely defrosted.* In a custard cup melt 1 tablespoon *butter or margarine* at **HIGH** for 45 seconds; stir in ½ teaspoon *paprika*. Brush the cornish hen well with some of the butter mixture. Place the hen, breast side down, on a microwave roasting rack in 8x8x2-inch baking dish. Cover with a loose tent of waxed paper. Cook at **MEDIUM HIGH or COOK POWER 7 (70%)** for 6 minutes. Then turn hen breast side up and brush again with the butter mixture. Continue cooking at **MEDIUM HIGH or COOK POWER 7 (70%)** for the remainder of the cooking time or till a meat thermometer* inserted in the center of inside thigh muscle, not touching bone, registers 180° to 185°F. Cover with foil and let it stand on counter for 5 minutes before serving.
	2 (1¼ pounds each)	24 minutes at **MEDIUM HIGH or COOK POWER 7 (70%)**	*Make sure hens are completely defrosted.* In a custard cup melt 2 tablespoons *butter or margarine* at **HIGH** for 45 seconds; stir in ½ teaspoon *paprika*. Brush hens well with some of the butter mixture. Place hens, breast side down, on microwave roasting rack in a 12x7½x2-inch baking dish. Cover with loose tent of waxed paper. Cook at **MEDIUM HIGH or COOK POWER 7 (70%)** for 12 minutes. Turn the hens breast side up and give dish a half turn. Brush again with the butter mixture. Continue cooking at **MEDIUM HIGH or COOK POWER 7 (70%)** for the remainder of cooking time or till a thermometer* inserted in the center of the inside thigh muscle, not touching bone, registers 180° to 185°F. Cover the hens with foil and let them stand on counter for 5 minutes before serving.

*Do not use a conventional thermometer inside the microwave oven. Special microwave thermometers are available. Do not use a microwave meat thermometer in a conventional oven.

COMBINATION TURKEY ROASTING CHART

COMBINATION	WEIGHT	TOTAL COOKING TIME	METHOD

For a beautifully browned bird that doesn't take all day in the oven, try a combination microwave-conventional oven method. For charcoal-grilled flavor, use the combination microwave cooking and conventional grilling method.

COMBINATION	WEIGHT	TOTAL COOKING TIME	METHOD
Microwave and Conventional Ovens	8 pounds	40 minutes at **HIGH,** then 45 to 60 minutes in a 350°F oven	*Make sure turkey is completely defrosted.* In small bowl melt 2 tablespoons *butter or margarine* at **HIGH** for 45 seconds. Stir in 1 teaspoon *paprika;* set aside. Tie legs together and wings close to body. Cover legs and wings with foil; secure with wooden toothpicks. Place turkey, breast down, on microwave- and conventional oven-safe roasting rack in 12x7½x2-inch baking dish. Brush bird with some of butter mixture. Cover with loose tent of waxed paper. Cook turkey at **HIGH** for 15 minutes. Remove foil from legs. Turn turkey breast side up; brush with butter mixture. Cover; cook turkey **HIGH** for 15 minutes. Give dish a half turn. Insert a *microwave* meat thermometer* in center of inside thigh muscle, not touching bone. Cook, covered, at **HIGH** for remainder of microwave cooking time or till thermometer* registers 140°F. Remove waxed paper and remaining foil. Insert *conventional* meat thermometer* in center of inside thigh muscle, not touching bone. Place turkey in conventional 350°F oven and cook for 45 to 60 minutes or till thermometer* registers 180° to 185°F. Let stand 15 minutes before carving. If any portion of turkey is not quite done, slice and return just that portion to the microwave oven and cook at **MEDIUM HIGH or COOK POWER 7 (70%)** for a few minutes.
Microwave Oven and Grill	8 pounds	40 minutes at **HIGH,** then 45 to 60 minutes on a covered grill	*Make sure turkey is completely defrosted.* In small bowl melt ¼ cup *butter or margarine* at **HIGH** for 1 minute. Stir in 2 teaspoons *paprika,* ½ teaspoon *salt,* ¼ teaspoon *pepper,* and ¼ teaspoon *poultry seasoning.* Rub over cavity of turkey. Tie legs together and wings close to body. Cover legs and wings with foil; secure with wooden toothpicks. Place turkey, breast down, on microwave roasting rack in 12x7½x2-inch baking dish. Brush with butter mixture. Cover with loose tent of waxed paper. Cook turkey at **HIGH** for 15 minutes. Remove foil. Turn turkey, breast up and give dish a half turn. Brush again with some of the butter mixture. Cover; cook turkey at **HIGH** for 15 minutes. Give dish a half turn. Insert *microwave* meat thermometer* in center of inside thigh muscle, not touching bone. Cook at **HIGH** for remaining microwave cooking time or till thermometer* registers 140°F. Meanwhile prepare the grill: Arrange *medium* coals around a large foil drip pan in firebox of a covered grill. As soon as thermometer* registers 140°F in turkey thigh, place turkey on grate over drip pan. Remove microwave meat thermometer. Insert a *conventional* meat thermometer* in center of inside thigh muscle without touching bone. Lower grill cover. (Heat should be medium-slow above the drip pan.) Grill over *medium-slow* coals about 1 hour or till thermometer* registers 180° to 185°F, adding more coals as needed. Cover turkey with foil. Let stand 15 minutes before carving.

*Do not use a conventional thermometer inside the microwave oven. Special microwave thermometers are available. Do not use a microwave meat thermometer in a conventional oven.

Fish & Seafood

Choose fish or seafood for a change of pace in family menus. Delicate-textured foods such as fish and seafood stay moist and tender when cooked in the microwave oven. And whether you want a fast tuna casserole or elegant poached salmon steaks, turn to this chapter for easy and delicious entrées in just minutes.

Variety & servings

Add variety to your menus by including a fish dish often. Fish has a delicate flavor and tender texture. It's versatile and also cooks quickly. Popular varieties of fish include catfish, perch, cod, haddock, flounder, sole, halibut, red snapper, sea and striped bass, trout, salmon, and tuna.

Popular shellfish types include shrimp, lobster, crab, oysters, clams, scallops, and mussels.

To determine how much to buy, remember that an average serving consists of about 12 ounces whole fish, 8 ounces dressed or pan-dressed fish, 4 to 5 ounces fillets or steaks, or about 4 ounces fish sticks.

Cooking doneness

Test fish for cooking doneness by inserting the tines of a fork into the middle of the fillet at a 45° angle. The fish is done if it breaks away, or flakes, when the fork is gently twisted.

Fish pieces

Depending upon the recipe, fish fillets can be cut into a variety of sizes. Small, uniform-shaped fish pieces will cook faster and more evenly than large, uneven fillets. Small fish pieces are commonly used in soup and stew recipes, while larger portions are cooked in flavorful sauces or simply basted with a seasoned butter mixture.

Defrosting

A 1-pound block of fish fillets may be quickly defrosted in the package following the times recommended in the defrosting chart on pages 32-34. Separate the fillets for more even thawing.

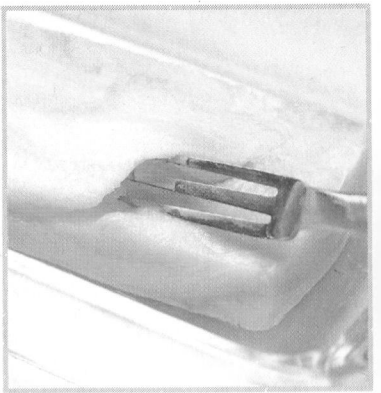

Buttered fish fillets

Place 1 pound of thawed fish fillets in baking dish, with thick portions to outside. If pieces are uneven, fold under small ends to make pieces of equal thickness. Drizzle fish with about 3 tablespoons seasoned butter mixture. Cook at Medium High or Cook Power 7 (70%) for 5 to 6 minutes or till fish flakes when tested.

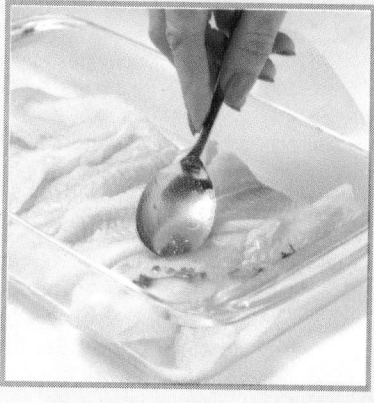

Poached steaks

Place 4 fish steaks (about 1½ pounds, cut 1 inch thick) in a 12x7½x2-inch baking dish. Add ¼ cup water. Cook, covered, at Medium High or Cook Power 7 (70%) for 12 minutes or till fish flakes easily when tested, giving dish a half turn twice.

Baked whole fish

Place 1¼ - to 1½-pound dressed whole fish in melted butter in 12x7½x2-inch baking dish. Cover; cook at Medium High or Cook Power 7 (70%) for 15 minutes till fish flakes when tested, giving dish a half turn once.

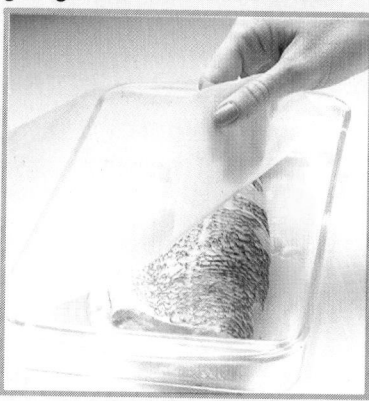

Breaded fish portions

Place frozen breaded fish portions, or fish sticks, on a plate lined with paper towel. Cook, uncovered, at High for 3 to 4 minutes or till heated through. *Or,* use a preheated 10-inch browning dish, following directions on page 17, Chapter 1.

FILLETS & STEAKS

BASIC BUTTERED FISH

Total cooking time: 5 minutes, 40 seconds

- 1 16-ounce package frozen fish fillets
- 1 tablespoon butter or margarine
  Sauce Amandine (optional)
  Sauce Devilish (optional)
  Salt

Thaw fish according to defrosting directions on page 34. Cut fish crosswise into 4 equal portions. Heat butter in 8x8x2-inch baking dish at **HIGH** for 40 seconds till melted. Stir Sauce Amandine or Sauce Devilish mixture into butter, if desired. Place fish portions in the seasoned butter mixture, turning to coat both sides. Sprinkle fish with some salt. Cook, covered with waxed paper, at **HIGH** for 5 minutes till fish flakes easily when tested with a fork, rotating dish twice. Makes 4 servings.

Sauce Amandine: Stir 1 tablespoon *lemon juice,* dash *salt,* and dash *pepper* into butter in baking dish. Cook fish as directed above. Before serving, remove fish from dish and stir 2 tablespoons toasted, slivered *almonds* and 2 teaspoons snipped *parsley* into juices in baking dish. To serve, spoon sauce over fish.

Sauce Devilish: Stir 3 tablespoons *chili sauce,* ½ teaspoon *prepared mustard,* ½ teaspoon *Worcestershire sauce,* ½ teaspoon *prepared horseradish,* and dash *salt* into butter in baking dish. Cook fish as directed above. To serve, spoon sauce over fish.

HAWAIIAN FILLETS

Total cooking time: 8 minutes, 30 seconds

- 1 pound fresh or frozen fish fillets
- ¼ cup packed brown sugar
- 1 tablespoon cornstarch
- 1 8-ounce can pineapple chunks
- ½ medium green pepper, cut into thin strips
- ¼ cup vinegar
- 1 tablespoon soy sauce
- 1 teaspoon snipped chives
  Dash garlic powder
- ¼ cup toasted sliced almonds

Thaw fish, if frozen, according to directions on page 34. In 2-cup glass measure combine brown sugar and cornstarch. Drain pineapple, reserving juice. Stir pineapple juice into brown sugar-cornstarch mixture. Stir in green pepper, vinegar, soy sauce, chives, and garlic powder. Cook at **HIGH** for 3½ minutes till thickened and bubbly, stirring after every minute. Stir in pineapple chunks; set aside. In 12x7½x2-inch baking dish arrange fish fillets, placing thicker portions toward outside of dish. Cover with waxed paper and cook at **HIGH** for 5 minutes till fish flakes easily when tested with fork, giving dish a half turn after 3 minutes cooking time. With slotted spatula, remove fish to serving platter. Spoon pineapple mixture over fish. Sprinkle with toasted almonds. Makes 4 servings.

FISH IN BEER BATTER

Total cooking time: 9 minutes

- 1 beaten egg yolk
- ½ cup packaged biscuit mix
- ⅓ cup beer
- ⅛ teaspoon salt
- 2 8-ounce fresh pan-dressed fish
- 1 tablespoon cooking oil

Preheat 10-inch browning dish at **HIGH** for 4 minutes. In pie plate beat together egg yolk, biscuit mix, beer, and salt till smooth. Pat fish with paper toweling to dry. Dip fish in batter to coat both sides. Add oil to preheated browning dish. Add fish. Cook at **HIGH** for 3 minutes. Turn; cook at **HIGH** for 2 minutes till done. Makes 2 servings.

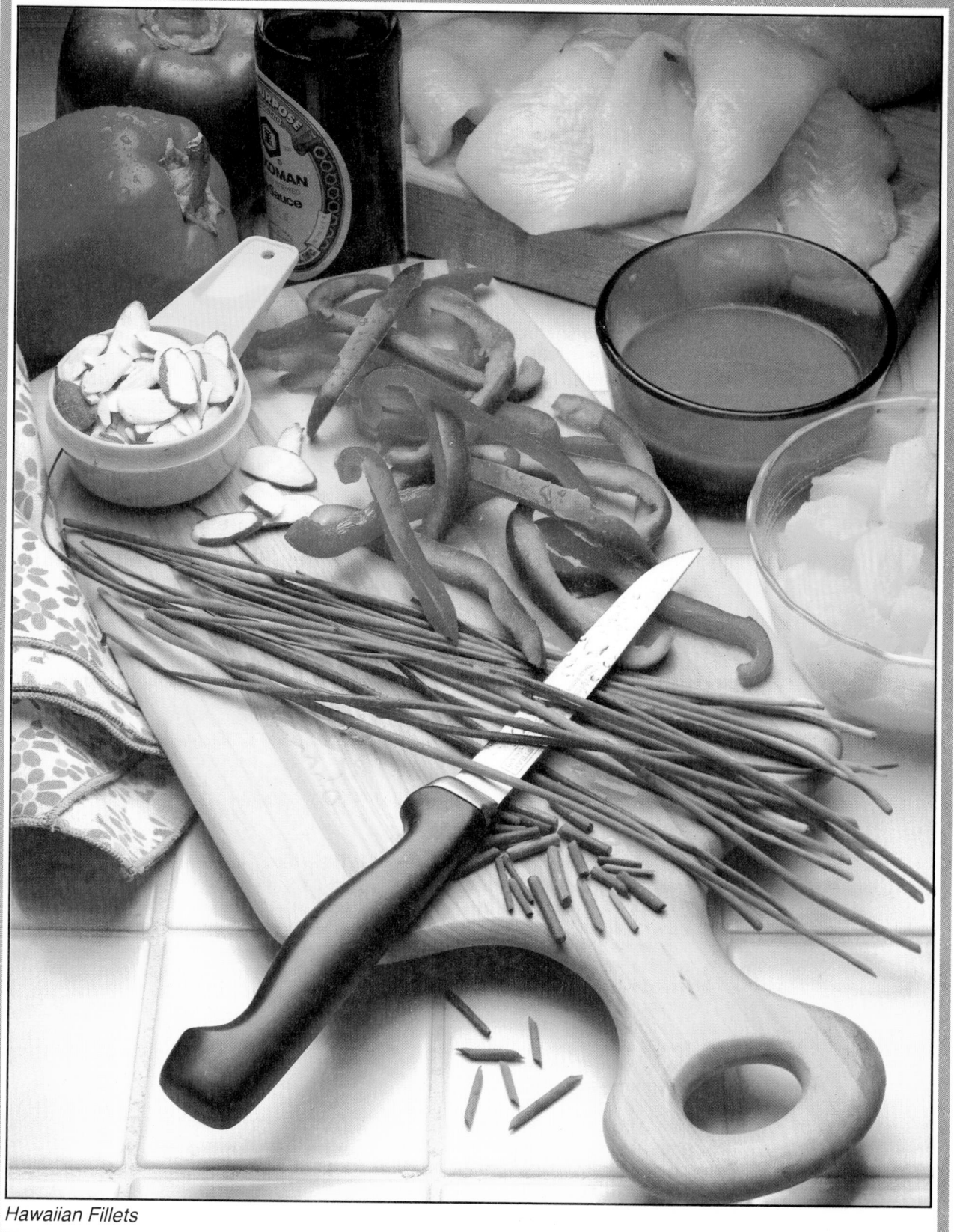

Hawaiian Fillets

FILLETS & STEAKS

HADDOCK ITALIANO

Total cooking time: 8 minutes

- 1 **pound fresh or frozen haddock fillets**
- ¼ **teaspoon dried basil, crushed**
  Dash salt
- 2 **tablespoons chopped onion**
- 1 **tablespoon water**
- ½ **of 16-ounce jar (1 cup) spaghetti sauce with mushrooms**
- ½ **cup shredded mozzarella cheese**

Thaw haddock fillets, if frozen, according to directions on page 34. Place fillets in 8x8x2-inch baking dish. Sprinkle with the basil and salt. In small bowl combine onion and water. Cover and cook at **HIGH** for 1½ minutes till tender. Sprinkle over fish fillets. Pour spaghetti sauce over fish fillets. Cover with waxed paper; cook at **HIGH** for 6 minutes till fish flakes easily when tested with a fork, giving dish a half turn twice. Top fish with shredded cheese; cook at **HIGH** for 30 seconds till the cheese melts. Makes 4 servings.

HADDOCK ROLL-UPS PROVENÇALE

Total cooking time: 15 minutes

- 1½ **to 2 pounds fresh or frozen haddock fillets (6)**
  Salt
  Paprika
- ¼ **cup chopped onion**
- 1 **clove garlic, minced**
- 1 **tablespoon butter or margarine**
- 2 **small tomatoes, peeled, seeded, and chopped**
- 1 **3-ounce can chopped mushrooms, drained**
- ½ **cup dry white wine**
- 2 **tablespoons snipped parsley**
- 1 **teaspoon instant vegetable bouillon granules**
- 1 **teaspoon sugar**
- 2 **tablespoons cold water**
- 2 **teaspoons cornstarch**

Thaw fish, if frozen, according to directions on page 34. Separate fish into fillets. Sprinkle one side of each fillet with a little salt and paprika. Roll up fillets; secure with wooden toothpicks. In a small bowl com-bine the onion, garlic, and butter. Cook at **HIGH** for 2 minutes till tender. In a 10x6x2-inch baking dish combine the onion mix-ture, tomatoes, mushrooms, wine, parsley, bouillon, and sugar. Cook at **HIGH** for 5 minutes till boiling, stirring once. Add fish roll-ups; cover and cook at **MEDIUM HIGH or COOK POWER 7 (70%)** for 5 minutes till fish flakes easily when tested with a fork. Remove to serving platter. Cover to keep warm. In small bowl combine water and cornstarch. Stir into vegetable mix-ture. Cook at **HIGH** for 3 minutes till mix-ture is thickened and bubbly, stirring twice. Spoon sauce over fish rolls. Serves 6.

CORN-STUFFED FILLETS

Total cooking time: 10 minutes

- 4 **fresh or frozen sole or haddock fillets (about 1 pound)**
- 1 **cup coarsely crumbled corn bread**
- 1 **cup soft bread crumbs (1½ slices)**
- ½ **cup fresh cooked or canned corn, drained**
- ¼ **cup chopped celery**
- 2 **tablespoons finely chopped onion**
- 1 **tablespoon finely chopped green pepper**
- ½ **teaspoon salt**
- ½ **teaspoon ground sage**
  Dash pepper
- 2 **tablespoons butter or margarine, melted**
- 1 **tablespoon water**

Thaw fish, if frozen, according to directions on page 34. In a medium mixing bowl com-bine corn bread, bread crumbs, corn, cel-ery, onion, green pepper, salt, sage, and pepper. Add melted butter and water, toss-ing lightly to coat. Place corn stuffing on boned side of fillets, dividing mixture evenly between fillets. Roll up fillets, securing each with a wooden toothpick. Place fish rolls in a 10x6x2-inch baking dish. Cover with waxed paper and cook at **MEDIUM HIGH or COOK POWER 7 (70%)** for 10 minutes till fish flakes easily when tested with a fork, giving dish a half turn once. Makes 4 servings.

Defrosting shrimp

For shelled shrimp, defrost according to the defrosting directions given on page 34, separating the pieces as necessary.

Boiled shrimp

Thaw shelled shrimp, if frozen. In a 1½- or 2½-quart casserole combine 1 cup water and 1 teaspoon seafood seasoning. Cook, uncovered, at High for 3 minutes or till mixture is boiling. Add shrimp; cook at High for 5 minutes till mixture returns to a boil. Cook at Medium or Cook Power 5 (50%) for 4 minutes or till shrimp are done. Cover; let stand 3 to 5 minutes. Drain to serve. Makes 6 servings.

Steaming clams

To prepare clams for steaming, first wash thoroughly. Then combine 1 gallon water and ⅓ cup salt in a large kettle or bowl. Add clams and let stand for 15 minutes; rinse well. Repeat soaking and rinsing two more times.

Place clams in single layer in oven cooking bag set in a shallow baking dish. Bring ½ cup water to boiling in a 1-cup glass measure; pour over clams. Tie loosely with string for steam to escape. Cook clams at Medium or Cook Power 5 (50%) for 7 to 8 minutes, turning the dish once. Loosen clams from shells; discard any clams that do not open.

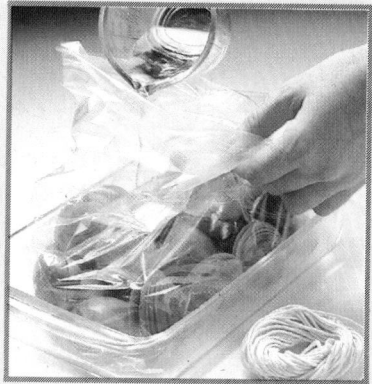

Defrosting lobster

Place an 8-ounce frozen lobster tail in an 8x8x2-inch baking dish. Defrost according to the defrosting directions on page 34. Test the tail for thawing doneness by bending the shell and checking for flexibility.

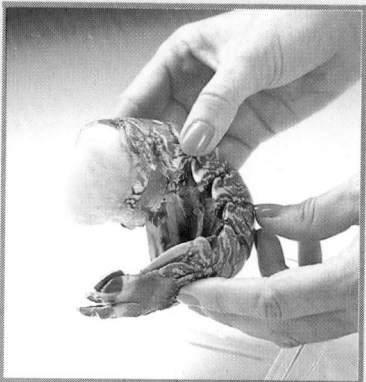

FRESH & FROZEN SEAFOOD

RED SNAPPER VERACRUZ

Total cooking time: 13 minutes

- 1 **pound fresh or frozen red snapper fillets, skinned**
- 1 **small tomato, peeled, seeded, and chopped**
- ¼ **cup chopped onion**
- ¼ **cup chopped green pepper**
- 2 **tablespoons butter or margarine**
- 2 **tablespoons chili sauce**
- 1 **tablespoon snipped parsley**
- 1 **tablespoon capers**
- 1 **tablespoon lemon juice**
- 1 **clove garlic, minced**
- ½ **teaspoon dried thyme, crushed**
  Several dashes bottled hot pepper sauce
- 1 **4½-ounce can small shrimp, rinsed and drained**
- ¼ **cup dry white wine**

Thaw fish, if frozen, according to directions on page 34; set aside. In 12x7½x2-inch baking dish combine tomato, onion, green pepper, butter, chili sauce, parsley, capers, lemon juice, garlic, thyme, and hot pepper sauce. Cover with waxed paper and cook at **HIGH** for 6 minutes till onion is tender. Stir in shrimp and wine. Place fish fillets atop, overlapping thin edges of fillets; spoon some of the sauce over fish. Cover and cook at **HIGH** for 7 minutes till fish flakes easily when tested with a fork, giving dish a half turn after 4 minutes. Makes 4 servings.

CREOLE-STYLE SHRIMP

Total cooking time: 20 minutes

- 1 **pound fresh or frozen medium shrimp in shells**
- ½ **cup chopped onion**
- ½ **cup chopped green pepper**
- ½ **cup chopped celery**
- 1 **clove garlic, minced**
- 2 **tablespoons olive oil or cooking oil**
- 2 **teaspoons cornstarch**
- 1 **8-ounce can tomato sauce**
- ½ **cup dry red wine or water**
- ¼ **cup catsup**
- 1 **bay leaf**
- 1 **tablespoon dried parsley flakes**
- ⅛ **teaspoon dried oregano, crushed**
- ⅛ **teaspoon dried thyme, crushed**
  Dash crushed red pepper
  Hot cooked rice

Thaw shrimp, if frozen, according to directions on page 34. Peel and devein the shrimp. In 2-quart casserole combine onion, green pepper, celery, garlic, and oil. Cook at **HIGH** for 4 minutes till tender, stirring after 2 minutes. Stir cornstarch into vegetable mixture till smooth. Add tomato sauce, red wine or water, catsup, bay leaf, parsley flakes, oregano, thyme, and red pepper. Cover and cook at **HIGH** for 3 minutes. Stir; cook at **MEDIUM or COOK POWER 5 (50%)** for 8 minutes till thickened and bubbly, stirring after 4 minutes. Add shrimp. Cook at **MEDIUM or COOK POWER 5 (50%)** for 5 minutes till done, stirring after 2½ minutes. Cover and let stand for 4 minutes. Serve over rice. Makes 4 servings.

SHRIMP-PINEAPPLE TOSS

Total cooking time: 9 minutes

- 1 **8-ounce package frozen cooked shrimp**
- 1 **8-ounce can pineapple tidbits (juice pack)**
- 1 **tablespoon cornstarch**
- 2 **tablespoons soy sauce**
- 8 **green onions, sliced diagonally into 1½-inch lengths**
- 1 **tablespoon cooking oil**
- 1 **teaspoon grated fresh gingerroot**
- 1 **8-ounce can sliced water chestnuts, drained**
  Hot cooked rice or chow mein noodles (optional)

Place shrimp under cool running water till partially thawed; set aside. Drain pineapple, reserving juice. Combine reserved pineapple juice and cornstarch; stir in soy sauce. Set aside. Place onions, oil, and gingerroot in 1½-quart casserole. Cook, uncovered, at **HIGH** for 3 minutes till tender, stirring once. Stir in soy mixture and water chestnuts. Cook, uncovered, at **HIGH** for 4 minutes till thickened and bubbly, stirring after each minute. Stir in shrimp and pineapple. Cook, covered, at **HIGH** for 2 minutes till heated through, stirring once. Serve with hot cooked rice or chow mein noodles, if desired. Makes 3 or 4 servings.

Eggs & Cheese

Eggs and cheese add delicious high-protein, low-cost variety to your family's menus. Cook fluffy scrambled eggs or melt a cheese topping in seconds in your microwave; but that's just the beginning. Add savory toppings to scrambled eggs, hearty fillings to omelets, or serve rich and saucy casseroles for tasty breakfast or light supper entrées.

Tips & Techniques

Making fried eggs

Fried eggs are best cooked in the 10-inch browning dish. Preheat the browning dish at High for 2 minutes. Add 1 tablespoon oil and carefully break the eggs into the preheated dish. Pierce the yolk membrane with a fork to prevent bursting during cooking. Add 1 tablespoon water; cover and cook at High for 1 to 1½ minutes or to desired doneness.

Making scrambled eggs

Combine the eggs, milk, and seasonings in a 10-ounce custard cup or cereal bowl; beat with a fork. Add butter. Cook, uncovered, according to time in chart at right.

Stir the cooked egg at the edges toward the uncooked egg

in the center of dish once or twice during the cooking time specified.

Stir scrambled eggs again before serving. Eggs should be slightly moist, not dry, when cooked. (Eggs continue to cook slightly in the few seconds it takes to serve.)

Making poached eggs

Pour 1 cup hot water into a 1-quart casserole. Cook, uncovered, at High for 2 to 3 minutes till boiling. Gently break the desired number of eggs into water and push to center of the dish. Pierce yolk membrane with a fork. Cover; cook at High for cooking time specified in the chart at right.

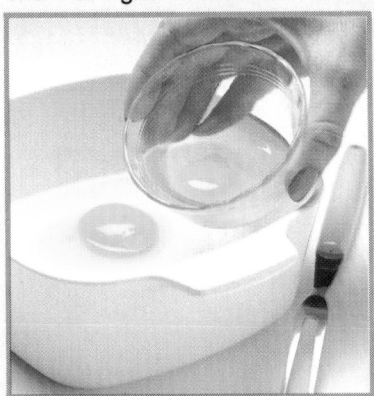

BASIC 2-EGG OMELET

Total cooking time: 3 minutes

- 2 **slightly beaten eggs**
- 2 **tablespoons water**
- ⅛ **teaspoon salt**
  Dash pepper
- 1 **teaspoon butter or margarine**
  Desired omelet filling, topping, and garnish (page 80)

Preheat 10-inch browning dish at **HIGH** for 1 minute. Meanwhile, combine eggs, water, salt, and pepper. Add butter or margarine to dish and tilt to coat. Pour in egg mixture and cover with browning dish lid. Cook at **HIGH** for 2 minutes till center is set but moist, rotating dish a quarter turn turn every 30 seconds. Spoon desired filling onto half the omelet. Roll or fold using pancake turner. Slide onto serving plate. Add filling, topping, and garnish as desired. Makes 1 serving.

Basic 3-Egg Omelet: Prepare egg mixture as above, preheating a 10-inch browning dish at **HIGH** for 1 minute and adding 1 teaspoon *butter or margarine.* Combine 3 *eggs,* 3 tablespoons *water,* ¼ teaspoon *salt,* and dash *pepper.* Cover and cook as directed as above at **HIGH** for 3½ minutes.

EGG FOO YUNG CASSEROLES

Total cooking time: 7 minutes, 30 seconds

- 1 **tablespoon butter or margarine**
- 2 **teaspoons cornstarch**
- 1 **teaspoon sugar**
- ½ **cup water**
- 4 **teaspoons soy sauce**
- ¼ **cup sliced green onion**
- ¼ **cup chopped celery**
- ¼ **cup chopped green pepper**
- 1 **tablespoon butter or margarine**
- 6 **beaten eggs**
- 1 **cup bean sprouts**
- ¼ **cup chopped water chestnuts**

In 2-cup glass measure heat 1 tablespoon butter at **HIGH** for 30 seconds. Stir in cornstarch and sugar. Add water and soy sauce. Cook at **HIGH** for 1½ minutes till thickened and bubbly, stirring twice. Cover to keep warm; set aside. In medium bowl combine green onion, celery, green pepper, and 1 tablespoon butter. Cover; cook at **HIGH** for 2½ minutes till crisp-tender. Stir in eggs, bean sprouts, and water chestnuts. Divide among four 12-ounce casseroles. Cook at **HIGH** for 3 minutes till eggs are set, giving casseroles a half turn once. Spoon some sauce mixture over each casserole. Makes 4 servings.

POACHED EGGS

Combine 1 cup hot water and ½ teaspoon vinegar in a 1-quart casserole. Cook, uncovered, at HIGH for 2 to 3 minutes till boiling. Gently break eggs into water; push to center of dish. Cover and cook at HIGH for time specified in chart below.

Number of Eggs	Time at HIGH	Let Stand (covered in the water)
1	1 minute	1½ to 2 minutes
2	1¼ minutes	2 minutes
4	2 minutes	2 minutes

FLUFFY SCRAMBLED EGGS

To cook 1 or 2 eggs, use a cereal bowl or a 10-ounce custard cup. To cook 4 to 6 eggs, use a 1-quart bowl. In bowl combine eggs, milk, and salt and pepper to taste; beat with fork. Add butter or margarine. Cook, uncovered, at HIGH and stir occasionally according to the chart. Stir before serving.

Number of Eggs	Milk	Butter	Minutes	Stir
1	1 tablespoon	1 teaspoon	¾ to 1¼	once
2	2 tablespoons	2 teaspoons	1¾ to 2¼	once
4	¼ cup	4 teaspoons	3½ to 4	twice
6	⅓ cup	2 tablespoons	5 to 6	twice

MUSHROOM-CHEESE PUFF

Total cooking time: 14 minutes, 30 seconds

- ½ cup sliced fresh mushrooms
- 2 tablespoons sliced green onion
- 2 tablespoons butter or margarine
- 1 tablespoon all-purpose flour
- ½ cup milk
- 1 tablespoon snipped parsley
- ¼ teaspoon salt
    Dash pepper
- 2 tablespoons butter or margarine
- 2 tablespoons all-purpose flour
- ¼ teaspoon salt
- ¼ teaspoon dry mustard
    Dash ground red pepper
- ½ cup milk
- 1 cup shredded cheddar cheese
    (4 ounces)
- 2 egg yolks
- 2 egg whites

For mushroom sauce, in 2-cup glass measure combine sliced mushrooms, green onion, and 2 tablespoons butter or margarine. Cook, uncovered, at **HIGH** for 2 minutes. Stir in 1 tablespoon flour. Add ½ cup milk, parsley, ¼ teaspoon salt, and pepper. Cook, uncovered, at **HIGH** for 2½ minutes, stirring after 1 minute. Cover and set aside.

In 4-cup glass measure place 2 tablespoons butter or margarine. Cook at **HIGH** for 30 seconds till melted. Stir in 2 tablespoons flour, ¼ teaspoon salt, the mustard, and ground red pepper. Add ½ cup milk and cook at **HIGH** for 1½ minutes till thickened and bubbly, stirring after one minute. Add shredded cheddar cheese; stir till melted. In small mixer bowl beat egg yolks for 3 to 4 minutes at high speed of electric mixer. By hand, add cheese mixture to egg yolks, stirring constantly. Cool mixture slightly. Wash beaters well. In large mixer bowl beat egg whites till stiff peaks form. Gently pour yolk mixture over whites; fold gently. Pour mixture into ungreased 3-cup soufflé dish. Cook, uncovered, at **MEDIUM or COOK POWER 5 (50%)** for 8 minutes. (Mixture will puff high, then fall.) Serve at once with mushroom sauce. Makes 2 servings.

ONION QUICHE

Total cooking time: 27 minutes

- 8 slices bacon
- 1 9-inch baked pastry shell
- 1½ cups thinly sliced onions,
    separated into rings
- 2 tablespoons butter or margarine
- 1 tablespoon all-purpose flour
- 1½ cups light cream or milk
- 2 cups shredded Swiss cheese
- 4 slightly beaten eggs
    Ground nutmeg (optional)

Cook bacon according to chart on page 51. Drain bacon and crumble into pastry shell; set aside. In a 1½-quart casserole place onions and butter. Cook, uncovered, at **HIGH** for 7 minutes till tender, stirring once. Stir in flour, ⅛ teaspoon *salt,* and ⅛ teaspoon *pepper.* Stir in cream. Cook, uncovered, at **HIGH** for 4 minutes till bubbly, stirring after each minute. Place cheese and eggs in large mixing bowl. Gradually stir hot cream-onion mixture into cheese and eggs. Pour warm egg-cheese mixture over bacon layer. Sprinkle with nutmeg, if desired. Cook, uncovered, at **MEDIUM HIGH or COOK POWER 7 (70%)** for 11 minutes, giving dish quarter turn every 2 minutes till center is nearly set. (Center will be soft-set and creamy.) Let stand for 5 minutes before serving. Makes 6 servings.

EGGS AND HASH

Total cooking time: 7 minutes

- 1 15-ounce can corned beef hash
- 4 eggs
    Pepper
- ¼ cup shredded cheddar cheese
    (1 ounce)
- ½ teaspoon snipped chives

Divide hash among four 6-ounce custard cups; spread evenly over bottoms and sides. Break 1 egg into each cup of hash; prick each egg yolk with tines of fork. Sprinkle with pepper. Cover; cook at **HIGH** for 6½ minutes till eggs are just done, rearranging cups once. Sprinkle cheese and chives over eggs; rearrange cups. Cook at **HIGH** for 30 seconds till cheese melts. Makes 4 servings.

Vegetables

All the best qualities of vegetables are retained when they're cooked in your microwave oven. They keep their vitamins, bright color, fresh flavor, and texture. This chapter is brimming with fast vegetable recipes and cooking tips to help you make tasty meal accompaniments. And, you'll find an easy-to-read vegetable cooking chart for quick reference.

Vegetables

Special Helps

Tips & Techniques

Cooking frozen vegetables

Place the vegetable carton or pouch on a plate. Make an X-shaped slit in the carton top or puncture the pouch with a fork to allow for the escape of steam. Cook according to directions given in the vegetable cooking charts on pages 85-90.

Cutting into equal pieces

Fresh vegetables will cook more evenly when they are cut into uniform sizes and shapes. Irregular-shaped pieces have a tendency to overcook and become mushy in spots while other areas may require additional cooking time.

Peeling tomatoes

Here's an easy way to prepare whole tomatoes for peeling.

In a 2-cup glass measure or medium bowl bring 1 cup water to boiling. Remove dish from microwave oven. Spear a tomato with a long-tined meat fork. Submerge the tomato in the hot water; hold to count of twelve. Hold the tomato under cold running tap water; peel.

Piercing to cook

Pierce skins of vegetables such as potatoes, sweet potatoes, and winter squash with a fork before cooking to vent steam during cooking.

Whole vegetables such as sweet potatoes and summer squash should be arranged in a spoke pattern for cooking, leaving a 1-inch space between each portion. Or, arrange stalks of fresh vegetables toward outside of the dish, tender parts toward center.

Steaming vegetables

Vegetables cooked in the microwave have a steamed, crisp-tender quality. Most vegetables are cooked covered, using the baking dish lid, vented plastic wrap, or waxed paper, so little water is needed. Chart times are for crisp-tender vegetables. Allow 5 minutes standing time to finish cooking. Add more time for a more tender vegetable.

Cooking whole vegetables

Large vegetables, such as cauliflower, can easily be cooked whole in the microwave oven. Remove outer leaves and the excess part of the stem. Place in a 1½-quart casserole with about 2 tablespoons water. Cover; cook according to the times given in charts on pages 85-90.

Cooking spinach

To cook leafy vegetables, such as spinach or collard greens, wash and trim leaves. Place the greens in a large casserole. The water that clings to the leaves will be adequate moisture for cooking.

Soaking dried beans

To eliminate overnight soaking of dried beans, rinse beans thoroughly. In 3- or 5-quart casserole combine beans and amount of water directed for soaking. Cook at High till boiling. Cover; let stand 1 hour. Drain, replacing volume of drained water with equal volume of fresh water. Continue cooking as directed in your favorite recipe or in charts on pages 85-90.

TWICE-BAKED POTATOES

Total cooking time: 25 minutes

   6 **potatoes**
   3 **tablespoons butter or margarine**
   ¾ **teaspoon salt**
      Dash pepper
   ¾ **cup milk**
      Paprika

Prick potatoes with tines of fork. Cook at **HIGH** for 16 minutes. Wrap with foil; let stand 5 minutes. Slice off and discard the top of each potato. Scoop out inside of each potato to make 6 shells. In large bowl combine the scooped-out potato, butter, salt, and pepper. Mash, adding enough milk to make fluffy consistency. Spoon mashed potatoes into the potato shells. Place stuffed potatoes on serving plate; sprinkle with paprika. Cook at **HIGH** for 2 minutes. Give dish a half turn and cook at **HIGH** for 2 minutes till potatoes are heated through. Garnish with snipped parsley or chives, if desired. Makes 6 servings.

Note: If desired, stuff potatoes ahead and refrigerate. Cook at **HIGH** for 8 minutes, giving dish a half turn after 4 minutes.

HERBED NEW POTATOES

Total cooking time: 18 minutes, 30 seconds

   1½ **pounds new potatoes**
   2 **cups water**
   2 **tablespoons butter or margarine**
   2 **teaspoons lemon juice**
   1 **tablespoon snipped parsley**
   1 **tablespoon snipped chives**
   ½ **teaspoon dried dillweed**

Peel a strip around center of each potato, if desired. In 2-quart casserole combine potatoes, water, and ½ teaspoon *salt*. Cover and cook at **HIGH** for 9 minutes. Stir; continue cooking potatoes at **HIGH** for 9 minutes till tender. Drain; set potatoes aside. In the same casserole combine butter, lemon juice, snipped parsley, snipped chives, dillweed, dash *salt,* and dash *pepper*. Cook at **HIGH** for 30 seconds till butter melts. Add potatoes; toss to coat. Makes 6 servings.

White Rice

In a 1½-quart casserole combine 2 cups water, 1 cup long grain rice, and ¾ teaspoon salt. Cook, covered, at HIGH for 5 minutes till boiling. Cook at MEDIUM LOW or COOK POWER 3 (30%) for 12 minutes or until tender. Cover and let stand for 5 minutes before serving.

ORANGE-GLAZED SWEET POTATOES

Total cooking time: 6 minutes

   ¼ **cup packed brown sugar**
   1 **tablespoon orange-flavored instant breakfast drink powder**
   2 **teaspoons cornstarch**
   ½ **cup cold water**
   3 **tablespoons butter or margarine**
   1 **18-ounce can sweet potatoes, vacuum-packed**

In 1½-quart casserole combine brown sugar, orange drink powder, cornstarch, and water. Cook at **HIGH** for 2 minutes till mixture is thickened and bubbly, stirring after 1 minute. Stir in butter. Add potatoes, stirring to coat. Cook at **HIGH** for 4 minutes till heated through, turning each potato over once. Makes 4 servings.

SPINACH NOODLE CASSEROLE

Total cooking time: 18 minutes

   ½ **cup finely chopped onion**
   2 **tablespoons butter or margarine**
   1 **clove garlic, minced**
   3 **cups (4 ounces) green noodles, cooked and drained**
   8 **hard-cooked eggs, chopped**
   2 **cups small-curd cream-style cottage cheese (16 ounces)**
   ⅓ **cup grated Parmesan cheese**
   1 **teaspoon Worcestershire sauce**
      Dash bottled hot pepper sauce
   ½ **cup dairy sour cream**
      Poppy seed
      Grated parmesan cheese

In 2-quart casserole combine onion, butter and garlic. Cook at **HIGH** for 3 minutes till onion is tender, stirring once. Add noodles and hard-cooked eggs. In a blender container combine cottage cheese, ⅓ cup Parmesan cheese, Worcestershire sauce, hot pepper sauce, and ½ teaspoon *salt*. Cover; blend smooth. Fold into the noodle mixture. Cover; cook at **MEDIUM HIGH** or **COOK POWER 7 (70%)** for 15 minutes till hot, stirring twice. Stir in sour cream; sprinkle with poppy seed. Pass grated Parmesan cheese. Makes 6 servings.

COOKING VEGETABLES

VEGETABLE	AMOUNT	WEIGHT	METHOD	TIME AT HIGH
Artichokes Fresh, Whole	1	10 ounce	Wash; remove stem and cut 1 inch from top. Brush cut edges with lemon juice. Cook in covered 2-quart casserole or wrap in waxed paper.	4 to 5 minutes
	2		Same as above.	6 to 7 minutes
Frozen, Hearts		9 ounces	Cook in covered 1-quart casserole with 2 tablespoons water. Stir once.	5 to 6 minutes
Asparagus Fresh, Spears	12 to 15	8 ounces	Wash spears and cut off tough end. Leave spears whole or cut into 3- to 4-inch lengths. Cook in a covered 1-quart casserole with 1/4 cup water. Rearrange once during cooking.	3 to 4 minutes
	30	1 pound	Same as above except use 2-quart casserole.	7 to 8 minutes
Frozen, Spears, Whole or Cut	1 1/2 cups	10 ounces	Cook in covered 1- or 1 1/2-quart casserole. Rearrange or stir once during cooking.	8 to 10 minutes
Beans Fresh, Green or Wax	3 cups	1 pound	Wash and remove ends. Leave whole or cut into 1- to 2-inch pieces. Place in 1 1/2-quart casserole with just enough water to cover. Cook, covered, rearranging or stirring once during cooking.	16 to 17 minutes
			To steam: Place washed whole or cut beans in 1 1/2-quart casserole with 1/4 cup water. Cook, covered, till crisp-tender, stirring or rearranging once.	10 to 11 minutes
Frozen, Green or Wax, French-style or Cut	1 2/3 cups	9 ounces	Cook in covered 1-quart casserole with 2 tablespoons water. Stir once.	10 to 12 minutes
Frozen, Italian Green	1 1/2 cups	9 ounces	Cook in covered 1-quart casserole with 2 tablespoons water. Stir once.	6 to 8 minutes
Frozen, Lima, Baby or Large	1 1/2 to 1 3/4 cups	10 ounces	Cook in covered 1-quart casserole with 1/4 cup water. Stir once during cooking.	9 to 10 minutes
Dried, Lima	1 cup	8 ounces	Rinse and presoak beans overnight in 3 cups water. Drain off soaking water. Bring 1 quart fresh water to boiling; add to beans in 3- to 5-quart casserole. Cook, covered, at **MEDIUM OR COOK POWER 5 (50%).** Stir once during cooking.	45 minutes at **MEDIUM or COOK POWER 5 (50%)**

COOKING VEGETABLES

VEGETABLE	AMOUNT	WEIGHT	METHOD	TIME AT HIGH
Beans Dried, Navy	1 cup	8 ounces	Same as for dried lima beans.	60 minutes at **MEDIUM or COOK POWER 5 (50%)**
Dried, Pinto	1 cup	8 ounces	Same as for dried lima beans.	45 minutes at **MEDIUM OR COOK POWER 5 (50%)**
Beets Fresh, Whole	6 medium (2 cups)	1 pound	Cut off all but 1 inch of stem and root. Wash; don't pare. Cook in covered 2-quart casserole with ½ cup water. Stir once during cooking. Peel when done.	18 to 20 minutes
Fresh, Sliced or Diced	6 medium (3 cups)	1 pound without leaves (1½ pounds with leaves)	Cut off all but 1 inch of stem and root; wash and pare. Slice or cube. Cook in covered 1½-quart casserole with ¼ cup water. Stir once during cooking.	11 to 12 minutes
Broccoli Fresh, Whole		1 pound	Wash and remove outer leaves and tough parts of stalks. Split stalks almost to bud. Cook whole in covered 2-quart casserole with ¼ cup water. Turn or rearrange once.	7 to 9 minutes
Fresh, Cut	4 to 5 cups	1½ pounds	Same as above except cut in 1½- to 2-inch pieces. Use covered 1½-quart casserole with ¼ cup water and stir once.	10 to 12 minutes
Frozen, Whole or Chopped		10 ounces	Cook in covered 1½-quart casserole with 2 to 3 tablespoons water. Stir or rearrange once during cooking.	8 minutes
Brussels Sprouts Fresh	4 cups (30)	1 pound	Cut off wilted leaves. Wash. Halve large sprouts. Cook in covered 1½-quart casserole with 2 tablespoons water; stir once.	8 to 9 minutes
Frozen		10 ounces	Cook in 1-quart covered casserole with 2 tablespoons water. Stir once.	9 to 10 minutes
Cabbage Fresh, Wedges	6 wedges	1½-pound head	Remove wilted outer leaves before cutting in wedges. Cook in covered 2-quart casserole with 2 tablespoons water. Rearrange once during cooking.	10 to 12 minutes
Fresh, Shredded	4½ cups	1 pound	Same as above except remove core before shredding. Cook in a covered 1½- or 2-quart casserole with 2°tablespoons water. Stir once during cooking.	10 to 12 minutes

COOKING VEGETABLES

VEGETABLE	AMOUNT	WEIGHT	METHOD	TIME AT HIGH
Carrots Fresh, Sliced or Diced	6 to 8	1 pound	Wash and peel; slice ½ inch thick or cut into ⅜-inch cubes. Cook in a covered 1½-quart casserole with ¼ cup water. Stir once during cooking.	10 to 12 minutes
	4	8 ounces	Same as above except cook in covered 1-quart casserole with 2 tablespoons water.	6 to 7 minutes
Frozen, Cut	2 cups	10 ounces	Cook in covered 1-quart casserole with 2 tablespoons water. Stir once.	6 to 7 minutes
Cauliflower Fresh, Whole	1	1 pound	Wash; remove outer leaves. Cook in covered 1½-quart casserole with 2 tablespoons water.	7 to 9 minutes
Fresh, Broken into Buds	6 cups	1 pound	Same as above but break into buds. Stir once during cooking.	7 to 8 minutes
Frozen		10 ounces	Cook in covered 1-quart casserole with 2 tablespoons water, stirring once during cooking.	7 to 8 minutes
Celery Fresh, Sliced	6 stalks (4 cups)	1 pound	Remove the leaves and root end. Wash and slice. Cook in a covered 1½-quart casserole with 2 tablespoons water, stirring once during cooking.	11 to 13 minutes
Corn on the Cob Fresh	1 ear	7 ounces	Remove husks and silk; rinse. Wrap in waxed paper, twisting ends to close. Or, arrange on plate or in baking dish covered with waxed paper.	2 to 3 minutes
	Additional ears		Same as above.	Add 2 to 3 minutes per ear
Frozen	1 ear		Same as above.	4 to 5 minutes
	Additional ears		Same as above.	Add 2 to 3 minutes per ear
Corn Fresh, Whole Kernels	3 ears (2 cups, cut)		Rinse; cut from cob. Cook in covered 1-quart casserole with 2 tablespoons water. Stir once during cooking.	5 to 6 minutes
Frozen		10 ounces	Cook in covered 1-quart casserole with 2 tablespoons water. Stir once.	6 to 7 minutes

COOKING VEGETABLES

VEGETABLE	AMOUNT	WEIGHT	METHOD	TIME AT HIGH
Eggplant Fresh	1 medium	1¼ pounds	Pare and cube or slice; cook in covered 2-quart casserole with 2 tablespoons water. Stir once during cooking.	4 to 5 minutes
Mixed Vegetables Frozen	2 cups	10 ounces	Cook in covered 1-quart casserole with 2 tablespoons water. Stir once.	8 to 10 minutes
Okra Frozen, Whole		10 ounces	Cook in covered 1-quart casserole with 2 tablespoons water. Stir once.	7 to 9 minutes
Onions Fresh, Quartered	3 or 4 large	1 pound	Peel and quarter. Cook in covered 1½-quart casserole with 2 tablespoons water. Stir once during cooking.	9 to 11 minutes
Frozen, Small Whole	2 cups		Cook in covered 1-quart casserole. Stir once during cooking.	5 to 6 minutes
Peas Fresh, Green, Shelled	2 cups	2 pounds	Wash. Cook in covered 1-quart casserole with 2 tablespoons water.	7 to 8 minutes
	3 cups	3 pounds	Same except use 1½-quart casserole.	9 to 10 minutes
Frozen, Green	2 cups	10 ounces	Cook in covered 1-quart casserole. Stir once during cooking.	5 to 6 minutes
Frozen, Black-eyed		10 ounces	Cook in covered 1-quart casserole with ½ cup water. Stir once.	12 to 13 minutes
Pea Pods Frozen		6 ounces	Make slit in pouch and place on plate or in bowl. Cook; rearrange once.	3 to 4 minutes
Potatoes Baked	1 whole	6 to 8 ounces	Scrub; prick skin with fork. Arrange in spoke pattern, leaving 1 inch space between. Cook till slightly firm. Wrap in foil. Let stand 5 minutes.	4 to 6 minutes
	Additional potatoes		Same as above.	Add 2 to 3 minutes per potato
Boiled Halves	3 medium	1 pound	Peel and halve. Cook in covered 1½- to 2-quart casserole with 1 cup water. Stir once.	11 to 13 minutes
	4 to 5 medium	1½ pounds	Same as above.	14 to 16 minutes

COOKING VEGETABLES

VEGETABLE	AMOUNT	WEIGHT	METHOD	TIME AT HIGH
Potatoes Baked Sweet or Yams	1 whole	5 to 6 ounces	Scrub; prick with fork. Arrange in spoke pattern, leaving 1 inch space between. Cook till slightly firm. Wrap in foil. Let stand 5 minutes.	5 to 6 minutes
	Additional potatoes		Same as above.	Add 2 to 4 minutes per potato
Boiled Halves	3	1 pound	Peel and halve. Cook in covered 1½- to 2-quart casserole with 1 cup water. Stir once.	10 to 11 minutes
Spinach Fresh	12 cups	1 pound	Wash thoroughly to remove sand particles. Trim off any bruised portions. Cook in covered 2-quart casserole. Stir once.	5 to 7 minutes
Frozen		10 ounces	Cook in 1½-quart covered casserole. Stir once during cooking.	6 to 8 minutes
Winter Squash Fresh, Whole Acorn	2	8 ounces each	Wash thoroughly. Prick skin in 2 or 3 places with a fork. Cook whole, rearranging once during cooking. Cut in half and remove the seeds before serving.	5 to 7 minutes
Fresh, Whole Hubbard	1	1½ pounds	Wash thoroughly. Cut in half and remove the seeds. Cut each half into 2 to 3 pieces. Cook in a 2-quart covered casserole with ¼ cup water, rearranging once.	10 to 12 minutes
Frozen Hubbard		12 ounces	Cook in 1-quart covered casserole. Stir once during cooking.	6 to 8 minutes
Summer Squash Fresh, Yellow Crookneck or Zucchini	2 medium (4 cups)	8 ounces each	Wash and cut into ½-inch thick slices. Cook in a 1½-quart covered casserole with ¼ cup water, stirring once.	6 to 7 minutes
	2 small (2 cups)	4 ounces	Same as above except use 1-quart casserole and 2 tablespoons water. Stir once..	4 to 5 minutes
Frozen, Zucchini		10 ounces	Cook in covered 1-quart casserole. Stir once during cooking.	5 to 6 minutes
Succotash Frozen		10 ounces	Cook in covered 1-quart casserole with 2 tablespoons water. Stir once during cooking.	9 to 10 minutes
Turnips Fresh	4 medium	1 pound	Wash and cut off the outer skin. Cut into quarters. Cook in covered 1½-quart casserole with ½ cup water. Stir once during cooking.	12 to 14 minutes

BLANCHING FRESH VEGETABLES FOR FREEZING

Your microwave oven can be a real time-saver when preparing vegetables for the freezer. These tips will help you preserve the garden-fresh flavors successfully.
- Prepare vegetables as indicated on the chart in amounts specified. Add water, but no salt.
- Cook for the minimum time, then check for doneness. The vegetable should be evenly heated and have a bright color throughout. Continue cooking if needed, using maximum time on chart.
- Plunge immediately into ice water; chill for an amount of time equal to cooking time. Drain well and pat dry with paper toweling.
- Package vegetables in moisture-vaporproof ½-pint or 1-pint freezer containers or plastic freezer bags. Seal; label with contents and date.
- Freeze vegetables immediately at 0° or below. Spread packages out to freeze quickly; stack when frozen solid. Store at 0° for up to 12 months.

VEGETABLE	AMOUNT	WEIGHT	METHOD	TIME AT HIGH
Asparagus Spears	30 (2 cups)	1 pound	Wash; cut off tough ends. Cut spears into 1- to 2-inch lengths. Cook in covered 2-quart casserole with ¼ cup water, rearranging once during cooking.	2½ to 3½ minutes
Beans, Green or Wax	3 cups	1 pound	Wash; remove ends and cut in 1- to 2-inch pieces. Cook in covered 1½-quart casserole with ½ cup water, rearranging once.	3½ to 5½ minutes
Broccoli Spears		1 pound	Wash; remove outer leaves and tough parts of stalks. Split lengthwise into 1-inch stalks. Cook in covered 2-quart casserole with ½ cup water, rearranging once during cooking.	3 to 5 minutes
Carrots, Sliced	6 to 8	1 pound	Wash and peel; slice ½ inch thick. Cook in covered 1½-quart casserole with ¼ cup water, stirring once during cooking.	3½ to 5½ minutes
Cauliflower	1 head	1 pound	Wash; remove outer leaves. Cut into flowerets. Cook in covered 2-quart casserole with ½ cup water, stirring once during cooking.	3 to 5 minutes
Corn, Cut from Cob	2 cups (3 to 4 ears)	about 1 pound	Cook in covered 1-quart casserole with ¼ cup water, stirring once.	3 to 4 minutes
Peas, Green, Shelled	2 cups	2 pounds	Wash. Cook in covered 1-quart casserole with ¼ cup water, stirring once.	3 to 4½ minutes
Spinach	12 cups	1 pound	Wash and trim; cook in 2-quart casserole. (Do not add water.) Stir once.	2½ to 3½ minutes
Squash, Zucchini or Yellow Crookneck	2 medium (4 cups)	1 pound	Wash; slice ½ inch thick. Cook in covered 1½-quart casserole with ¼ cup water, stirring once during cooking.	3 to 4 minutes
Turnips	4 medium	1 pound	Wash, peel, and cube. Cook in covered 1½-quart casserole with ¼ cup water, stirring once during cooking.	2½ to 4 minutes

Convenience Foods

When minutes count, take advantage of convenience foods. Use these pages to help you save time and energy. Package sizes change frequently, so use the timing ranges given in these charts as guidelines. Begin with the shortest time and add seconds and minutes.

APPETIZERS & BEVERAGES

PRODUCT	PACKAGE OR SERVING SIZE	METHOD	TIME COOK POWER
Cheese Fondue	14 ounces	Remove from foil package; place in 1-quart casserole. Stir after each minute for the first 2 minutes, then every 45 seconds. Serve warm.	4¼ minutes **MEDIUM HIGH or COOK POWER 7 (70%)**
Presweetened Cocoa Mix	1 cup	Pour 6 to 8 ounces milk or water, as package directs, into a mug. Heat. Stir in 2 to 3 teaspoons cocoa mix.	2 minutes **HIGH**
	2 cups	Same as above, using two mugs.	3 minutes **HIGH**
	4 cups	Same as above, using four mugs.	5 minutes **HIGH**
Frozen Egg or Pizza Rolls	6 to 6½ ounces	Arrange frozen rolls on paper plate. Heat uncovered.	2 to 3 minutes **HIGH**
Vienna Sausages	5 ounces	Remove sausages from can; place on paper plate. Cook uncovered till heated through.	45 seconds **MEDIUM HIGH or COOK POWER 7 (70%)**

MAIN DISHES

Frozen Beef Burritos	5 ounces (1 burrito)	Remove from wrapper; heat on paper plate.	2 to 2½ minutes **HIGH**
	10 ounces (1 burrito)	Same as above, except give plate half turn after 2½ minutes.	4 to 5 minutes **HIGH**
	16 ounces (4 burritos)	Remove burritos from package. Heat on serving plate.	5 minutes **MEDIUM HIGH or COOK POWER 7 (70%)**
Frozen Stuffed Cabbage Rolls	14 ounces	Uncover foil pan; return foil pan to carton. Cook, giving pan a half turn after 9 minutes.	18 minutes **MEDIUM LOW or COOK POWER 3 (30%)** then 7 to 8 minutes **MEDIUM HIGH or COOK POWER 7 (70%)**

PRODUCT	PACKAGE OR SERVING SIZE	METHOD	TIME COOK POWER
Frozen Fried Chicken Pieces	16 ounces (5 or 6 pieces)	Remove the chicken pieces from container; arrange on a microwave roasting rack in a baking dish. Cook uncovered until thawed, turning pieces over and rearranging once.	6 minutes **MEDIUM LOW or COOK POWER 3 (30%)**
		Continue cooking uncovered till hot through, turning chicken over and rearranging once.	4 minutes **MEDIUM HIGH or COOK POWER 7 (70%)**
	25 ounces (5 to 7 pieces)	Remove chicken pieces from container; arrange on a microwave roasting rack in a baking dish. Cook uncovered until thawed, turning pieces over and rearranging once.	6 minutes **MEDIUM LOW or COOK POWER 3 (30%)**
		Continue cooking uncovered till hot through, turning chicken over and rearranging once.	12 minutes **MEDIUM HIGH or COOK POWER 7 (70%)**
	32 ounces (9 to 11 pieces)	Remove chicken pieces from container; place on microwave roasting rack in baking dish. Cook uncovered till thawed, turning pieces and rearranging once.	8 minutes **MEDIUM LOW or COOK POWER 3 (30%)**
		Continue cooking uncovered till hot through, turning chicken over and rearranging once.	15 minutes **MEDIUM HIGH or COOK POWER 7 (70%)**
Frozen Chicken Crepes Entrée	8¼ to 8½ ounces	Remove crepes from container. Place on serving plate. Cook.	3 minutes **MEDIUM LOW or COOK POWER 3 (30%)**
		Give plate a quarter turn. Puncture pouch with a fork in 2 places and place on plate with crepes. Continue cooking till heated through.	3 to 4 minutes **HIGH**
Frozen Dinner (3 courses)	7½ to 12½ ounces (in plastic tray)	Uncover tray; re-cover tray with vented plastic wrap or the plastic lid provided. (Do not return tray to carton.) Cook, turning tray once during cooking.	7 to 12 minutes **MEDIUM HIGH or COOK POWER 7 (30%)**
Frozen Scrambled Eggs and Sausage Breakfast	6¼ ounces	Remove tray from carton. Cut a 2-inch slit in oven film. Place tray on paper plate. Cook till hot.	3½ minutes **HIGH**
Frozen Entrée (in pouch)	5 ounces	Place pouch on paper plate. Cut a 1-inch slit in center of pouch. Cook till hot and bubbly.	3 minutes **HIGH**
	8 ounces	Same as above, except cut a 3-inch slit.	6 minutes **HIGH**

PRODUCT	PACKAGE OR SERVING SIZE	METHOD	TIME COOK POWER
Hamburger Dinner Mix	7¼ to 8½ ounces	Crumble hamburger in a 2-quart casserole. Cook uncovered, stirring 3 times.	5 minutes **HIGH**
		Drain off fat. Add mix and ingredients as package directs (subtract ½ cup water, if desired). Cover and cook, stirring twice.	15 to 20 minutes **MEDIUM or COOK POWER 5 (50%)**
Macaroni and Cheese Mix	7¼ to 8 ounces	Cook macaroni conventionally on range top as package directs. Drain and place in 1½-quart casserole. Add ingredients as package directs. Cook covered, stirring once.	3 to 4 minutes **HIGH**
Frozen Macaroni and Cheese	7 or 12 ounces	Uncover foil pan. Cook uncovered, stirring mixture after 5 minutes.	9 minutes **HIGH**
Canned Meat-Vegetable Mixture	8 ounces	Spoon into small serving bowl. Cook covered till heated through, stirring once.	2 minutes **HIGH**
	15 ounces	Same as above.	4 minutes **HIGH**
Frozen Omelets with Cheese Sauce (in paper tray)	7 ounces	Remove tray from carton. Cut a 2- to 3-inch slit in oven film. Place tray on paper plate. Cook, giving tray a quarter turn after 3 minutes.	6 minutes **MEDIUM HIGH or COOK POWER 7 (70%)**
Oriental Dinner (divider pack)	42 ounces total (2 cans)	In 1½-quart casserole heat contents of small can uncovered, stirring once.	3 minutes **HIGH**
		Drain vegetables from large can; add to casserole and cook covered, stirring once.	4 minutes **HIGH**
Canned Pasta in Meat or Tomato Sauce	14¾ to 15 ounces	Cook covered in 1-quart casserole. Let stand 2 minutes. Stir before serving.	3 minutes **HIGH**
	26 to 26½ ounces	Same as above.	4½ minutes **HIGH**
Pepper Steak Dinner Mix	29 to 29¾ ounces	In 2-quart casserole cook meat uncovered, stirring mixture 3 times.	5 minutes **HIGH**
		Drain off fat. Stir together sauce mix and water as package directs; add to casserole with drained vegetables. Cook uncovered till thickened, stirring after 3 minutes, then after each minute.	8 minutes **HIGH**
Frozen Sandwiches	9 ounces (2 sandwiches)	Place sandwiches on plate. Cook uncovered.	5½ to 6 minutes **MEDIUM LOW or COOK POWER 3 (30%)**
	1 sandwich	Same as above.	4 minutes **MEDIUM LOW or COOK POWER 3 (30%)**

PRODUCT	PACKAGE OR SERVING SIZE	METHOD	TIME COOK POWER
Frozen Cheese-Stuffed Shells	9 ounces	Uncover foil pan; re-cover pan with vented plastic wrap. Place in microwave oven.	4 minutes **MEDIUM HIGH or** **COOK POWER 7 (70%)**
		Stir sauce and spoon over shells; continue heating. Stir twice during last 6 minutes of heating time.	6 minutes **MEDIUM HIGH or** **COOK POWER 7 (70%)**
Spaghetti Dinner Mix	8 ounces	Cook spaghetti conventionally. In 4-cup glass measure combine dry sauce mix and ingredients as directed on package. Cook covered till boiling.	3 minutes **HIGH**
		Continue cooking covered. Serve over spaghetti.	5 minutes **MEDIUM or** **COOK POWER 5 (50%)**
	19½ ounces	Prepare as above, except pour sauce from can into 4-cup glass measure. Cook uncovered till heated through. Sprinkle with cheese.	2 to 3 minutes **HIGH**
Tuna Dinner Mix	7¾ to 9 ounces	Prepare mix using package oven method. Combine ingredients in a 2-quart casserole (subtract ¼ cup water, if desired). Cook covered, stirring twice.	15 to 20 minutes **MEDIUM or** **COOK POWER 5 (50%)**
		Continue cooking covered till hot.	3 minutes **HIGH**
Frozen Welsh Rarebit	10 ounces	Uncover foil tray; return foil tray to carton. Cook, stirring twice during cooking.	6 to 7 minutes **HIGH**

ACCOMPANIMENTS

PRODUCT	PACKAGE OR SERVING SIZE	METHOD	TIME COOK POWER
Dry Creamed Potatoes Mix	4¾ ounces	Heat 1¼ cups water in 2-quart casserole.	3 minutes **HIGH**
		Add 2 cups milk and sauce mix and potatoes from package. Cook covered, stirring 3 times. Let stand covered 5 minutes before serving.	20 minutes **MEDIUM or** **COOK POWER 5 (50%)**
Instant Mashed Potatoes	4 servings	In 1½-quart bowl combine ingredients (water, milk, butter, and salt) as package directs. Cook covered till boiling. Stir in instant potatoes. Let stand before serving, if package directs.	3¾ minutes **HIGH**
Dry Scalloped Potatoes Mix	5½ ounces	Heat 2½ cups water in a 2-quart casserole.	5 minutes **HIGH**
		Add milk and butter as package directs; stir in sauce mix and potatoes from package. Cook covered till potatoes are tender, stirring 3 times.	20 minutes **MEDIUM or** **COOK POWER 5 (50%)**
Noodles Romanoff Mix	5½ ounces	In 2-quart casserole combine noodles and sauce mix from package with 1½ cups water and ½ cup milk. Cook covered till noodles are tender, stirring 3 times. Let stand covered 5 minutes before serving.	18 minutes **MEDIUM or** **COOK POWER 5 (50%)**

PRODUCT	PACKAGE OR SERVING SIZE	METHOD	TIME COOK POWER
Minute-type Quick-cooking Rice	4 servings	In 1-quart casserole combine 1 cup water and salt. Cook uncovered till boiling. Stir in 1 cup rice. Let stand covered for 5 minutes. Fluff rice mixture with a fork before serving.	2½ minutes **HIGH**
Seasoned Quick-cooking Rice Mix	6¼ to 7 ounces	In 1½-quart casserole combine rice and seasonings from package. Stir in additions as directed on package. Cook uncovered till boiling. Let stand covered 10 minutes before serving.	6½ to 7 minutes **HIGH**
Seasoned Regular Rice Mix	6 ounces	In 2-quart casserole combine rice and additions as package directs. Cook covered till boiling, stirring once.	6 minutes **HIGH**
		Cook covered till tender, stirring twice. Let stand covered for 5 minutes.	12 minutes **MEDIUM or COOK POWER 5 (50%)**
Stuffing Mix	6 to 8 ounces	In 1½-quart casserole combine water and butter as package directs with seasoning packet. Cook covered till boiling. Continue cooking covered. Stir in stuffing crumbs and let stand 5 minutes. Fluff with a fork.	4 to 4½ minutes **HIGH** then 3 minutes **MEDIUM or COOK POWER 5 (50%)**
Canned Vegetables	8¼ to 8½ ounces	Pour undrained vegetables from can into bowl. Cover with waxed paper; cook till thoroughly heated. Drain.	2 minutes **HIGH**
	12 ounces	Same as above, stirring once.	2½ to 3 minutes **HIGH**
	16 ounces	Same as above, stirring once.	3½ minutes **HIGH**
Frozen Baked Stuffed Pototes	10 or 12 ounces	Place potatoes on serving plate. Cover with waxed paper. Turn plate once during cooking.	6 to 7 minutes **HIGH**
Frozen French-Fried Potatoes	16 ounces	Place on paper towel-lined plate or paper plate. Cook uncovered till hot. Potatoes will not be crisp.	6 minutes **HIGH**
Frozen Fried Potato Nuggets	16 ounces	Place on paper-towel-lined plate or paper plate. Cook uncovered till hot. Nuggets will not be crisp.	7 minutes **HIGH**
Frozen Rice (in Pouch)	12 ounces	Place pouch in bowl. Puncture top with fork 2 or 3 times. Give pouch a half turn during cooking.	7 to 8 minutes **HIGH**
Frozen Vegetables with Sauce Cubes	8 to 10 ounces	Place package contents in 1-quart casserole; add water as directed on package. Cook covered till sauce is thickened, stirring after 2 minutes.	5 to 5½ minutes **HIGH**
Frozen Vegetables with Sauce (in Pouch)	8 to 10 ounces	Place pouch in bowl. Puncture top 2 or 3 times with fork. Give pouch a half turn once during cooking.	6 to 8 minutes **HIGH**

BREADS

PRODUCT	PACKAGE OR SERVING SIZE	METHOD	TIME COOK POWER
Coffee Cake Mix	10½ ounces	Prepare batter as package directs. Spoon into ungreased 8-inch round baking dish. Cook uncovered, giving dish a half turn after 5 minutes.	11 minutes **MEDIUM or COOK POWER 5 (50%)**
	14 ounces	Same as above, except use a 8x8x2-inch baking dish and give dish a quarter turn twice.	16 minutes **MEDIUM or COOK POWER 5 (50%)** then 1½ to 2 minutes **HIGH**
Corn Bread Mix	10 ounces	Prepare batter as package directs. Spoon into ungreased 8-inch round baking dish. Cook uncovered, giving dish a half turn once.	10 minutes **MEDIUM or COOK POWER 5 (50%)**
	15 ounces	Same as above, except use 8x8x2-inch baking dish.	14 minutes **MEDIUM or COOK POWER 5 (50%)** then 1½ to 2 minutes **HIGH**
Nut Bread Mix	15 to 17 ounces	Prepare batter as package directs. Spoon into waxed paper-lined 9x5x3-inch loaf dish. Cook uncovered, giving dish a half turn once. Let stand for 10 minutes.	16 minutes **MEDIUM or COOK POWER 5 (50%)** then 2 minutes **HIGH**

SAUCES & GRAVIES

PRODUCT	PACKAGE OR SERVING SIZE	METHOD	TIME COOK POWER
Canned Sauce or Gravy	10½ to 13½ ounces	Heat uncovered in serving bowl, stirring once.	4 minutes **HIGH**
Sauce or Gravy Mix	Made with ⅔ cup liquid	In 2-cup glass measure combine dry mix and liquid as package directs. Cook uncovered till thickened and bubbly, stirring after 1 minute, then every 30 seconds.	2 minutes **HIGH**
	Made with 1 cup liquid	Same as above.	2½ minutes **HIGH**
	Made with 2 cups liquid	Same as above, except use a 4-cup glass measure.	7 minutes **HIGH**
Spaghetti Sauce Mix	1¼ to 2½ ounces	In 4-cup glass measure blend ingredients as package directs (tomato sauce or paste, water, and butter or oil). Cook uncovered till boiling. Stir after 3 minutes.	6 to 7 minutes **HIGH**
		Cover and cook, stirring once or twice.	10 minutes **MEDIUM or COOK POWER 5 (50%)**
Bottled or Canned Spaghetti Sauce	15 to 16 ounces	Heat uncovered in a 4-cup glass measure till hot.	4 to 5 minutes **HIGH**

CAKE MIXES

PRODUCT	PACKAGE OR SERVING SIZE	METHOD	TIME COOK POWER
One-Layer Mix	In 8x1½-round dish	Prepare batter as package directs. Spoon all 2¼ cups batter into baking dish. After 4 minutes give dish a half turn. Cool 10 minutes on flat surface; cool completely on wire rack.	8 to 9 minutes **MEDIUM or COOK POWER 5 (50%)** then 1 to 1½ minutes **HIGH**
Two-Layer Mix	In two 8x1½-inch round dishes	If cake is to be turned out of dish after baking, line dish with waxed paper. Prepare batter as package directs. Divide batter between two dishes, using 2¼ cups for each. Cook one at a time. After 4 minutes, give dish a half turn. Cool 10 minutes on flat surface; cool completely on wire rack.	8 to 9 minutes **MEDIUM or COOK POWER 5 (50%)** then 1 to 1½ minutes **HIGH**
	In 12x7½x2-inch dish	Prepare batter as package directs. Use only a scant 3 cups of the batter. After 7 minutes, give dish a half turn. Cool 10 minutes on flat surface; cool completely on wire rack. Use remaining batter for cupcakes.	14 minutes **MEDIUM or COOK POWER 5 (50%),** then 2 minutes **HIGH**
	In 10-inch tube or fluted dish	Grease and sugar dish. Prepare batter as package directs. Use all batter. After 5 minutes, give dish half turn. Let stand 10 minutes on flat surface, then invert on wire rack.	11 minutes **MEDIUM or COOK POWER 5 (50%)** then 4 to 5 minutes **HIGH**
Cupcakes or Muffins	1	Prepare batter as package directs. Spoon 2 tablespoons batter into 6-ounce custard cup lined with paper bake cup. Unused batter may be refrigerated for later use.	30 to 35 seconds **HIGH**
	2	Same as above except, use two custard cups lined with paper bake cups.	40 to 50 seconds **HIGH**
	4	Same as above except, use four custard cups or microwave muffin dish lined with paper bake cups. Rearrange custard cups or give muffin dish half turn after 40 seconds.	1¼ to 1½ minutes **HIGH**
	6	Same as above except, use six custard cups or microwave muffin dish lined with paper bake cups. Rearrange custard cups or give muffin dish half turn after 1 minute 10 seconds.	2 minutes, 25 seconds **HIGH**
Snack-type Cake Mix	14 to 15½ ounces in 8x8x2-inch dish	Prepare batter as package directs. Place 6-ounce custard cup in center of dish before adding batter. Use all of batter. After 5 minutes, give dish half turn.	10 minutes **MEDIUM or COOK POWER 5 (50%)**
		Continue cooking, giving dish a half turn once. Let stand 10 minutes on flat surface before serving.	1½ to 2 minutes **HIGH**
Pound Cake Mix	In two loaf dishes, each 9x5x3- or 8x4x2-inches	Prepare batter as package directs; divide between dishes. Cook one at a time, giving quarter turns every 3 minutes. Cool 10 minutes on flat surface; cool completely on wire rack.	10 to 11 minutes **MEDIUM or COOK POWER 5 (50%)**

PRODUCT	PACKAGE OR SERVING SIZE	METHOD	TIME COOK POWER
Gingerbread Mix	14 ounces in 8x8x2-inch dish	Prepare batter as package directs. Use all of batter. After 3 minutes, give baking dish a half turn. Cool 10 minutes on flat surface. If desired, cool completely on wire rack.	7 minutes **MEDIUM or COOK POWER 5 (50%)** then 2 to 2½ minutes **HIGH**
Brownie Mix	23¾ ounces in two 8x1½-inch round dishes	Prepare as package directs. Divide batter between dishes. Cook one dish at a time. Give quarter turns every 3 minutes. Cool 10 minutes on flat surface; cool completely on wire rack.	8½ minutes **MEDIUM or COOK POWER 5 (50%)**

DESSERTS

PRODUCT	PACKAGE OR SERVING SIZE	METHOD	TIME COOK POWER
Regular Pudding Mix	4-serving-size	In 4-cup glass measure combine mix and milk as package directs. Cook uncovered till thickened and bubbly, stirring every 2 minutes. Cool.	6 minutes **HIGH**
	6-serving-size	Same as above.	9 minutes **HIGH**
Frozen 2-Crust Pie (unbaked)	26 ounces	Remove from package. Cook uncovered in microwave oven. Then place on baking sheet bake in 450° conventional oven for 15 minutes, till evenly browned.	10 minutes **HIGH**
	37 ounces	Same as above.	12 to 13 minutes **HIGH**
Frozen Brownies	13 ounces	Uncover foil tray. Heat uncovered, turning tray once. Let stand 5 to 10 minutes before serving.	3½ minutes **LOW or COOK POWER 2 (20%)**
Frozen Frosted Cake	17 ounces (3-layers)	Remove from package. Heat uncovered on plate.	3½ minutes **LOW or COOK POWER 2 (20%)**
	12 ounces (1-layer)	Uncover foil tray. Place on plate; heat. Let stand 5 minutes.	3 minutes **LOW or COOK POWER 2 (20%)**
Frozen Cheesecake	17 ounces	Uncover foil tray before heating.	4 minutes **LOW or COOK POWER 2 (20%)**
Frozen Pound Cake	10¾ ounces	Uncover foil tray. Heat. Let stand 5 minutes.	4 minutes **LOW or COOK POWER 2 (20%)**
Fudge Mix	14 ounces	In 1-quart bowl place butter as directed on package. Heat till melted.	45 seconds **HIGH**
		Blend in fudge mix and water as package directs. Cook, stirring every 30 seconds. Pour into pan; let stand 10 minutes. Chill.	1½ minutes **HIGH**

Converting Recipes

Save time in the kitchen by adapting your long-time favorite conventional recipes to microwave cooking. Use these easy guidelines to help turn your conventional recipes into time-saving microwave ones. Then, turn the page—there's an easy, and delicious, recipe example for converting a pot roast recipe to micro-cooking!

Tips

Microwave cooking is a moist method of cooking food. The easiest foods to microwave-cook are those that are naturally moist, such as chicken, fish, ground beef, vegetables, and fruits. Other good choices are saucy main dishes and foods that are steamed, covered, or stirred during cooking.

Many micro-cooked foods do not develop a dry, crisp crust. If this is an important recipe feature, you should cook it conventionally. Casseroles can be given a crisp, brown surface by adding a crunchy topping after the final stirring.

To convert a conventional recipe, check this book for a similar recipe using the same type and approximate amount of solid main ingredient. For example, if you want to convert a conventional meat loaf made with 1 pound of ground beef, find a microwave recipe that calls for the same amount of meat. Use the microwave recipe as a guide to selecting a cooking utensil, cooking technique, cook power level, and cooking time.

What to change

Some recipes need no changes, other than microwave-safe cooking dish and reduced cooking time. Yet others require slight changes in the amounts of some ingredients due to the way microwaves work.

Cooking utensils: Remember to cook in oven-proof glass, or ceramic dishes without metal trim; or use cookware designed for microwave ovens. If you're not sure about a utensil, refer to the dish test on page 12.

Fats: Many conventional recipes call for fat to keep foods from sticking to the pan or dish. But when you micro-cook foods, you can eliminate fats or add just a tablespoon of butter, margarine, butter-flavored cooking oil, or olive oil for added flavor.

Liquids: Foods cooked in the microwave oven retain their moisture and usually cook so rapidly that little evaporation occurs. When converting a conventional recipe, reduce the liquid by about ⅓. Check frequently during cooking; add more liquid if the food appears a bit dry.

Seasonings: Microwave cooking brings out the natural flavor of food, so you may not want as much seasoning. Small amounts of herbs and spices need not be changed, but use slightly less salt and pepper. After cooking, adjust the seasoning to suit your taste.

Cooking time

The greatest change will occur in cooking time. Your best guide is a similar microwave recipe, but if you can't find one, try cutting the conventional time to ⅓ or ¼ of the total conventional cooking time. Test for cooking doneness frequently to prevent overcooking. If the food needs more cooking time, add it in small amounts.

POT ROAST WITH BUTTERMILK
GRAVY (CONVENTIONAL)

Total cooking time: about 2 hours

- 1 **3-pound beef chuck pot roast**
- 2 **tablespoons cooking oil**
  Salt and pepper
- 1 **cup water**
- 2 **teaspoons instant beef bouillon granules**
- 1 **teaspoon dried thyme, crushed**
- ½ **teaspoon dried rosemary, crushed**
- 2 **bay leaves**
- 3 **medium potatoes, peeled and sliced ½ inch thick**
- 1 **medium onion, cut into wedges**
- 1 **cup sliced carrots**
- ½ **cup buttermilk**
- ¼ **cup all-purpose flour**

In a large kettle or Dutch oven brown meat in hot oil slowly on all sides; drain off excess fat. Sprinkle with salt and pepper. Add water, bouillon granules, thyme, rosemary, and bay leaves. Cover and bake in 325° oven for 1½ to 2 hours. Add potatoes, onion, and carrots the last 15 minutes of roasting. Remove the meat and vegetables to warm platter; cover and keep warm. Skim fat from pan juices; remove bay leaves. Measure pan juices, adding water if necessary to make 1½ cups total liquid. In screw-top jar combine buttermilk and flour. Cover and shake well. Stir into pan juices. Cook and stir till thickened and bubbly. Cook 1 minute more. Season to taste with additional salt and pepper, if desired. Spoon some of the gravy over meat and vegetables; pass remaining. Makes 8 servings.

- Look for similar recipes on pages 55-58.

- *Oil for browning step may be eliminated.*

- *Browning is not necessary in the microwave, especially when roasts are cooked in browning bag.*

- *Combine the liquid and seasonings for even distribution of flavor in shorter cooking time.*

- *Total cooking time for meats is about one-third to one-half the conventional time.*

POT ROAST WITH BUTTERMILK
GRAVY (MICROWAVE)

Total cooking time: 55 minutes

- 1 **3-pound beef chuck pot roast**
  Salt
  Pepper
- 1 **cup water**
- 2 **teaspoons instant beef bouillon granules**
- 1 **teaspoon dried thyme, crushed**
- ½ **teaspoon dried rosemary, crushed**
- 2 **bay leaves**
- 3 **medium potatoes, peeled and sliced ½ inch thick**
- 1 **medium onion, cut into wedges**
- 1 **cup sliced carrots**
- ½ **cup buttermilk**
- ¼ **cup all-purpose flour**

Sprinkle roast with salt and pepper. Place roast in an oven cooking bag; set bag in 12x7½x2-inch baking dish. Combine water, bouillon granules, thyme, rosemary, and bay leaves. Add to roast in cooking bag. Tie loosely with non-metallic string to seal. Cook at **HIGH** for 5 minutes, then at **MEDIUM or COOK POWER 5 (50%)** for 20 minutes. Open bag; turn meat over. Add potatoes, onion, and carrots to bag atop meat. Spoon juices over vegetables. Seal bag as before. Cook at **MEDIUM or COOK POWER 5 (50%)** for 25 minutes till meat and vegetables are tender; remove to platter and keep warm. Skim fat from pan juices; remove bay leaves. Pour juices into 4-cup glass measure; add water, if necessary, to make 1½ cups total liquid. In screw-top jar combine buttermilk and flour; cover and shake well. Stir into pan juices. Cook at **HIGH** for 4 minutes till thickened and bubbly, stirring after every minute. Season to taste with additional salt and pepper. Spoon some of the gravy over meat and vegetables; pass the remaining. Makes 8 servings.

Bi-Level Meals

Your microwave oven is especially designed for bi-level cooking. This convenient feature lets you cook several foods at one time for a complete meal, so you can serve it at once—hot! Use these pages for tips on using your bi-level cooking rack and to create easy microwave meals.

If your microwave oven comes with a Bi-Level Cooking Rack, this chapter will teach you how to use the handy utensil with time-saving ease.

The bi-level cooking rack is a convenient space saver that allows you to cook several foods simultaneously. The cooking rack elevates the food to give you added space, allowing you to cook a combination of dishes together as a meal. When you're finished, remove the rack and it stores easily.

5. As a rule of thumb, figure the timing for foods that are cooked together in the microwave oven, using the bi-level rack, will be approximately the same as the sum of its parts. In other words, add together the total cooking time for each food as if each had been cooked separately.

6. Check foods often while they are cooking. Remove any foods that are done; cover and keep warm. Continue cooking till all foods are done, removing from the oven as necessary.

How to microwave foods together

1. Place the food that takes the longest to cook to the far right on the rack in the microwave oven.

2. Place the food with the shortest cooking time to the far left on the bottom of the microwave oven or directly below a dish on the top rack.

3. Leave space, if possible, between foods on the rack to allow energy to reach the foods on the bottom of microwave oven.

4. Add items that heat quickly, such as rolls, on the bottom of the microwave oven during the last few minutes of cooking time for the rest of the meal.

Dish size and fit

Several foods can be cooked at one time using the Bi-Level Cooking Rack. Check dish sizes and shapes to make sure they fit inside the oven. The rack has 2 positions to adjust to various heights of utensils or food.

Position of dishes

Place foods that take the longest to cook on the rack near the energy source, leaving proper space between foods. Some foods may be started or removed before others.

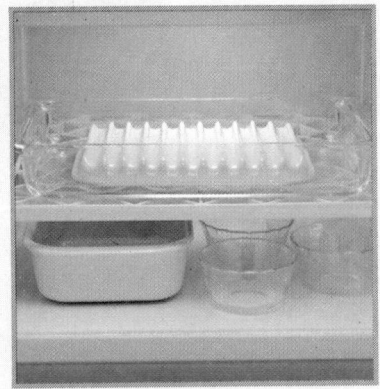

Simple breakfast

In a 10-ounce custard cup or cereal bowl combine 1 *egg*, 1 tablespoon *milk,* and *salt* and *pepper* to taste; beat with a fork. Add 1 tablespoon *butter or margarine.* Place 2 *precooked sausage links* on a folded paper towel and position to one side of dinner plate; put custard cup on plate. Set plate in the microwave oven. Cook at High for 1¾ minutes, stirring the egg once.

To warm coffee and coffee cake: Set an 8-ounce coffee mug of room temperature *coffee* in center of the bi-level rack. Wrap serving-size piece of *coffee cake* in a napkin and set on a small plate; position directly below coffee. Heat coffee and cake at High for 1¼ minutes.

Simple supper

Pour one 16-ounce can *pork and beans* into a 1-quart casserole. Cover; place to right side on bi-level rack. Place 4 *ground meat patties* in an 8x8x2-inch baking dish. Cover; place to left side of oven bottom. Cook at High for 5 minutes. Turn patties over and rearrange; stir beans. Cook at High for 5 minutes more till meat is almost done and beans are hot. Place 4 *hamburger buns* on piece of paper toweling on rack to the left side of the beans. Continue cooking at High for 1 to 1½ minutes more till hamburgers are cooked and beans and buns are heated through.

Soup and sandwich

Place 1 cup *soup* in bowl; position on bi-level rack. Cover loosely with waxed paper. Cook at High 2 minutes; stir soup. Wrap *frankfurter in bun* in a paper napkin; place below soup. Heat at High for 1½ to 2 minutes.

Index